BED
WED
BEHEAD

BED WED BEHEAD

Adam Nightingale

The History Press

To my brother, Mark.

First published 2014

The History Press
The Mill, Brimscombe Port
Stroud, Gloucestershire, GL5 2QG
www.thehistorypress.co.uk

British Library Cataloguing in Publication Data.
A catalogue record for this book is available from the British Library.

ISBN 978 0 7509 5611 6

Typesetting and origination by The History Press

Printed and bound in India by Nutech Print Services

CONTENTS

ACKNOWLEDGEMENTS

MY HEARTFELT THANKS TO THE FOLLOWING: Cate Ludlow, my frequent and brilliant collaborator from The History Press, who suggested this project and kept me on track, on time and (mostly) on topic. Tom and Rebecca Porritt, who were the first to play *Bed, Wed, Behead*. Mark Nightingale, my most excellent brother, to whom this book is dedicated, who laughed at all the good jokes, constructively sneered at all the bad ones and contributed the punchline to Captain Cook. My sister-in-law Susannah and my wonderful nephew Aeson. And my Mum and Dad, for reasons obvious and eternal to anyone who has had the privilege to meet them.

TWO WILLIAMS and a HENRY

William I

William II

Henry I

  Choose one to bed, one to wed and one to behead!

William I

Before his great victory at the Battle of Hastings, Norman warlord William the Conqueror was known as William the Bastard. This was entirely due to his dubious parentage, rather than any unpleasantness in his personality – though to be fair, that could be quite unpleasant too. William was fantastic husband material – so long as you were shorter than him. According to some sources, William was only 5ft 2in tall, whilst his wife Matilda (to whom he would remain faithful all his life) was 4ft 2in.

Despite being a super-fit Norman fighting machine, William was prone to putting on weight: when he died his pall-bearers could not fit his bloated corpse into his sarcophagus. Thus the first Norman King of England was born William the Bastard, but would die William the Fat Bastard.

William II

William was a red-faced blond with piercing blue eyes and a speech impediment. You would have known if a date with William was going well because he stammered when he was excited. But that would have been highly unlikely unless you were a burly Norman knight, given that William II was probably gay.

William had problems making friends. His brother hated him and most likely had him murdered. God didn't seem to like him very much either, causing the tower above William's tomb to collapse on top of his dead body (or so his subjects believed). A note for would-be dates: best avoid the New Forest.

Henry I

Henry was well-educated (he once said 'an illiterate king [is] a crowned ass'), a great diplomat and administrator and in his thirty-five year reign there was no rebellion on English soil. Yet he is the Norman king we know the least about. Having said that, we know that he probably became king by killing his brother Stephen (in a mysterious 'hunting accident'), and he definitely burnt out his other brother's eyes. Henry also threw an oath-breaker off the roof of Rouen Castle and blinded and mutilated his own grandchildren. He was notoriously unfaithful, with more than twenty illegitimate children (the most of any English king). On the plus side, if you are suffering from scrofula Henry I's your man – he was the first King of England divinely empowered to heal you. Interested?

A **STEPHEN**, a **HENRY** and a **RICHARD**

Stephen I

Henry II

Richard I

  Choose one to bed, one to wed and one to behead!

Stephen I

King Stephen (not to be confused with Stephen King) bears the distinction of being the only King of England named Stephen. Other than that, not an awful lot is remembered about him. He could be very chivalrous though. He once escorted Queen Matilda, his defeated rival to the English throne, across the country to Bristol. He could also be a bit of an idiot: Matilda repaid his generosity by stirring up the West of England against him, before defeating him and imprisoning him in Lincoln. King Stephen also wrote a best-selling book about a haunted hotel, a town filled with vampires, an angry psychic teenager – no, wait a minute …

Henry II

Ladies of more mature years are quids in: Henry loved those medieval cougars. Henry would marry the original MILF (Milady I'd Like to Foundadynastywith), Eleanor of Aquitaine. Sadly, Eleanor and Henry would fall out, plunging the Angevin Empire into years of bloody civil conflict. That said, Henry was something of a medieval 'new man' and certainly knew how to apologise: after accidentally causing the murder of his Archbishop of Canterbury and former BFF Thomas Becket, Henry expressed his shock and remorse by walking barefoot to Canterbury in sackcloth and ashes, where he was thrashed with whips by monks. Kinky!

Richard I

The golden boy of the Third Crusade, Richard conquered Cyprus and won an outstanding victory at Acre. However, he would never take Jerusalem – so you could say that Richard was not a finisher. Work took Richard away from home a lot: he would only spend six months of his ten-year reign in England, and wouldn't ever bother to learn English. But, on the positive side, Richard had a reputation for mercy (unless, of course, you were a Saracen – he beheaded 2,000 of them). Legend has it that when Richard received his death wound, at the Siege of Chalus, he was so impressed with the bravery of the man who shot him that he made his soldiers promise not to hang him. (They skinned him alive instead. Classic!)

Two **KINGS** of **ENGLAND** and a **FRENCH KING***

John

Henry III

Louis VIII

*who snuck in on a technicality

  Choose one to bed, one to wed and one to behead!

John

John had many negative points: he was not what you would call a family man, he rebelled against his father and his brother, and is strongly believed to have murdered his nephew. Neither was he what you might call a people person: John was excommunicated by the Pope, persecuted the Jews, hanged Welsh teenagers from the battlements of Nottingham Castle and antagonised his own nobles into forcing him to sign Magna Carta to curb his tyrannical excesses. John's positive qualities were … trying really hard … Sorry! Can't think of any.

Henry III

Although Henry was only 9 years old when his father, King John, died, he endeavoured to do all he could to honour the legacy of his dead dad. Unfortunately, this meant annoying the barons, antagonising the Church, accidentally strengthening the powers of Parliament, needling the French, making an enemy of the powerful Simon de Montfort and getting himself deposed. Thank goodness then for Edward, Henry's far more manly and kingly son, who restored his father's kingdom at the Battle of Evesham. If you are considering a date with Henry, you should know that you're probably better off with de Montfort: he was well fit. Oh, sorry, you can't – he was hacked to pieces at Evesham.

Louis VIII

King John was so unpopular that 700 English nobles invited the French monarch Louis to reign in his stead. Louis was actually quite a catch: he was brave (they called him 'The Lion'), virtuous, shrewd, self-controlled and religious. On second thoughts, though, the religious bit might cause you a few problems. If you are a Catharist (an extreme Gnostic aesthete who believes the Church in Rome is Satan's agent on earth), for example, then best give Louis a wide berth, lest he massacre you and 7,000 of your neighbours like he did at the Siege of Marmande. Other than that, you'll be fine.

Three **KINGS** Called **EDWARD**

Edward I

Edward II

Edward III

Choose one to bed, one to wed and one to behead!

Edward I

Wasn't this the king who executed Mel Gibson and threw his own son's boyfriend out the window in that movie? That's the one! Do you really want to go out with this man? Perhaps? On the plus side, you'd get to date a man known as 'the Hammer', which sounds promising. You might get to live in a nice castle too. Edward loved castles – he built them like they were going out of fashion. This was mainly to subjugate all those rebellious Celts like William Wallace and Llywelyn ap Gruffydd that he'd spend all his reign fighting. Actually, despite his warmongering reputation, England under Edward was the most stable it had been for generations. But then again, perhaps that's because if you betrayed him he'd have you hanged, drawn and quartered, a form of execution personally invented by Edward to kill Mel Gibson.

Edward II

The son of Edward I. In Edward II's case, the apple had fallen very far from the tree – Edward was not classic king material. For starters, Edward tended to lose things – like Scotland. Also, Edward did like his favourites: three was never a crowd on a date with Edward, so suitors should expect an attractive young nobleman named Piers or Hugh to accompany them at all times. But don't worry: if you ever feel like a gooseberry on your own date, be patient, as some faction of disgruntled noblemen will be bound to show up eventually and murder them all. Edward himself would perish in the worst of ways, having a red-hot poker shoved up his Ponder's End. In the immortal words of Lance Corporal Jones, 'They don't like it up 'em!'

Edward III

Edward was the greatest of all medieval English kings ever to have a pop at the French. However, Edward definitely had father issues: his own dad was murdered by having a heated spike shoved up his arse; in response, Edward had his stepfather hanged, drawn and quartered for usurping the throne. Consequently, anybody considering marrying Edward and starting a family must take into consideration the fact that Edward's own parenting style would inevitably be somewhat unorthodox. For example, at the Battle of Crécy, Edward refused to send aid to his son, the Black Prince, who was hemmed in by French knights. Unorthodox? Maybe. Effective? Definitely! The prince survived, learned independence and grew up to be the sort of self-sufficient killing machine that would make any parent proud.

A **KING**, a **PRINCE** and a Rather Powerful **DUKE**

Richard II

Edward,
the Black Prince

John of Gaunt

  Choose one to bed, one to wed and one to behead!

Richard II

Richard was a classic case of peaking too early: crowned king at 10; suppressed the Peasants' Revolt at 15; all downhill from there. The rest of Richard's reign was mired in civil war, rebellion, usurpation and death. But he did inspire a play by Shakespeare, the one with loads and loads of talking and hardly any fighting: 'Let us sit upon the ground, and tell sad stories of the death of kings.' Crikey … feeling sleepy …

Edward, the Black Prince

What a man, what a man, what a man, what a mighty mighty good man! Won his spurs at Crécy aged 16. Captured the French king at Poitiers, aged 17. The great hero of the first leg of the Hundred Years' War. Heir to the throne of England. Inspired the annual school diversity celebration 'Black Prince History Month'. Unfortunately, Edward would never rule. He would predecease his father and die of some disease he picked up in Spain. If you think it might have been cool dating someone known as the Black Prince, think again – Edward was never called the Black Prince in his lifetime. He was known as Edward of Woodstock. Not so cool – unless you like Crosby, Stills and Nash.

John of Gaunt

Son of Edward III. Brother to the Black Prince. Guardian of Richard II. John of Gaunt inspired one of the most patriotic speeches William Shakespeare ever wrote: 'This royal throne of kings, this sceptred isle, this earth of majesty …' But it's hard to see why: yes, John of Gaunt was one of the richest and most powerful men in fourteenth-century England, but he was also a bit of a seedy sexoholic. John would sire seven legitimate children over two marriages and four illegitimate children with his mistress Katherine Swynford (resulting in the accidental founding of the Tudor dynasty along the way). Gaunt may also have had syphilis. This infected begetter of kings, this sceptred letch, this dirty old man …

Bed

THE LOVE TRIANGLE between Charles II, Barbara Palmer and John Churchill played out like one of those seedy *Confessions* films popular in the 1970s, but with Grade I listed buildings as locations and much better diction.

Palmer was the king's most notorious mistress, who had given birth to five of his illegitimate children. Churchill, meanwhile, was a distant cousin of Palmer's. Churchill and Palmer had always been good friends but when young John returned from military service aged 20, all tanned and buff, friends soon became friends with royal benefits. Palmer and Churchill pretty much spent the next three years having sex.

Churchill was taking an enormous risk: Charles II, although happy to commit serial adultery whenever mood or opportunity took him, did not like to share his mistresses with his subjects. It was said that the king interrupted Churchill and Palmer on two occasions. The first interruption saw Churchill leaping out of Palmer's bedroom window and into the courtyard below. Churchill successfully evaded capture and was given £5,000 by Palmer as a thank-you gift. The second interruption saw the king, in response to a tip-off, burst in on Palmer, only to find her (apparently) alone: Churchill was hiding in the wardrobe. The king was no fool and extracted the cowering soldier from his closet. Churchill (who would go on to exhibit extraordinary courage as England's greatest general) grovelled and begged the king's forgiveness. Charles was said to have pardoned Churchill with the words, 'Go; you are a rascal, but I forgive you because you are doing it to get your bread,' which was the king's polite way of calling Churchill a man-whore.

THREE HENRYS

Henry IV

Henry V

Henry VI

  Choose one to bed, one to wed and one to behead!

Henry IV

Henry IV was best known for deposing his cousin Richard II on rather spurious genealogical grounds, starting the Wars of the Roses and then feeling guilty about it. Really guilty. Henry was all about the guilt: pressing, oppressive guilt. Henry was an insomniac. Why? Guilt! Henry paraded Richard II's dead body across the country. Why? Guilt! That, and the fact that he wanted his subjects to see that he hadn't stabbed, bludgeoned or garrotted his rival to the throne to death. He really hadn't. He starved him to death instead. But at least he felt guilty about it. (Ladies, take note: if Henry ever cheats on you he'd probably feel really guilty and tell you about it. If he ever asks you to try out a new diet, however, run for the hills.)

Henry V

Although principally famous for killing an awful lot of French people at the Battle of Agincourt, Henry was an all-round smooth operator. Everybody loved him: the Church, the barons and even the peasants (despite hiking taxes higher than the hated Richard II ever did). Smooth! To be fair to other less-popular monarchs, Henry did not live long enough to make any stupid mistakes: he expired at the age of 35. But ladies beware: though Henry lived fast and died young, he did not leave a good-looking corpse. Henry a) had half his face disfigured by a nasty arrow wound (which he was quite sensitive about), and b) died of an appalling case of dysentery. So a) don't request a forward-facing portrait on RoyalMatch.com, and b) take plenty of Imodium with you.

Henry VI

Dear, oh dear, oh dear! Henry VI accidentally restarted the Wars of the Roses, hastened the demise of the House of Lancaster and single-handedly lost the Hundred Years' War (and we were doing so well). Henry was prone to bouts of insanity and gloom, which may well have caused his death. (Alternatively, he may have been murdered in the Tower of London.) So, not exactly king material – unless by 'king' you mean '***king useless'.

MONARCHS of the WARS of the ROSES

Edward IV

Edward V

Richard III

  Choose one to bed, one to wed and one to behead!

Edward IV

The Wars of the Roses king Shakespeare couldn't be bothered to write a play about. Why? Don't know – Edward was awesome. He dressed like a male model, won two battles by the time he was 19, sorted out the economy, defeated his power-crazed uncle and drowned his treacherous brother in a vat of really expensive wine. But Edward did have one serious problem: he loved the ladies. All of them. Rich, poor, married, single – Edward was quite the amorous democrat, even jeopardising an alliance with France for a chance to get his leg over. In modern terms you might call him a sex addict. What's not to like, Bard of Avon?

Edward V

Bed, wed or behead? Edward V was 12 years old when he died, for goodness sake! What's wrong with you people?!

Richard III

Damn you, Shakespeare! Richard III was hardly the treacherous child-murdering social climber the Bard painted him as: Richard was fiercely loyal to his brother, Edward; a kind ruler to the people; he was religious, sexually temperate and a (largely) faithful spouse. In fact, anybody looking for good husband material could have done a lot worse. However, recent archaeological discoveries prove that Shakespeare was right about one thing: Richard's spinal abnormalities were genuine. The same recent discoveries have also proved that Richard spent an awful lot of time hanging around in a Leicester car park. On second thoughts, best keep him away from your kids.

TUDOR KINGS of ENGLAND

Henry VII

Henry VIII

Edward VI

  Choose one to bed, one to wed and one to behead!

Henry VII

After a really promising start, Henry VII's reign got boring very quickly. Following a spectacular victory over Richard III at Bosworth, Henry VII had only a few more rebellions to put down before his reign settled into a supremely dull stability as he rebuilt the economy, re-established strong trade links with former enemies, reformed the judiciary and left a healthy and wealthy England for his son and heir. However, Henry VII did broker a treaty with France called the 'Great Intercourse', which is quite funny. It sounds even ruder in Latin.

Henry VIII

Before he got monstrously fat, grew a red beard, accidentally formed a new religion, plundered numerous monasteries, killed virtually everyone who ever worked for him and two of his six wives, Henry VIII was actually a pretty decent guy. He was charismatic, clever, handsome, and more than 6ft tall; a sportsman who excelled at hunting, tennis and jousting, Henry was also the life and soul of any party, with a great love of banquets, jewellery, music (he played several instruments) and fancy dress. Still, probably best not to wed this one … Plus he'll end up looking like Sid James.

Edward VI

Was there even an Edward VI? Apparently there was. Edward VI was the only legitimate son of Henry VIII. On the pro side, ladies, Edward was a fan of 'bling': his clothes and even his books were encrusted with gold and jewels. He was clever, spoke three languages, and played the lute. On the slightly less attractive side, he was murderously cruel to his perceived enemies (ordering that Edinburgh, for example, be 'put all to fire and sword', as he preferred to put it). How come I didn't know any of that? Probably because Edward dropped dead shortly after his voice broke and his sisters were ten times more interesting.

Two **STUART KINGS** and One **REPUBLICAN** Gatecrasher

James I

Charles I

Oliver Cromwell

  Choose one to bed, one to wed and one to behead!

James I

Despite an odd appearance (he had skinny legs and a tongue too big for his mouth), James had a very high opinion of himself, taking the belief that he was answerable to God alone to new heights. Consequently he improved the title of the Bible by putting his own name on it, annoyed the Puritans and provoked the Catholics into trying to blow him up on Guy Fawkes Night (he really should have seen that one coming). But you've gotta love a man who shouts out 'I give not a turd for your preaching' at a bunch of Presbyterians. We've all wanted to do it.

Charles I

If you love nice art, then Charles is your man. He owned paintings by Titian and Raphael and was a patron to Rubens and Van Dyke. But his love of art did put undue strain on the royal purse, provoking the English Civil War; either that or something to do with Parliament v. the divine right of kings to do whatever they damn well please. But it was reported that when Charles was executed, his severed head carried on talking. How cool is that? So choose behead. Go on.

Oliver Cromwell

What's he doing here? He's not a king. He hated kings. As a Member of Parliament and staunch Puritan military genius, Cromwell deposed the reigning monarch in the English Civil War, had the king beheaded and then established himself as Lord Protector , a title he passed on to his son. That's 'Lord Protector'. Not 'King of England'. With Cromwell what you see is what you get. No doctored dating profile picture for this Puritan megalomaniac: Cromwell was an advocate of the 'warts and all' school of portraiture, commissioning a painting by Peter Lely that showed him as he was, with a face literally covered with warts. Good luck with that, Oliver.

Two More **STUART KINGS** and an **ORANGE** Representative

Charles II

James II

William III

  Choose one to bed, one to wed and one to behead!

Charles II

Having fled the country after losing the Second English Civil War and then losing the Second Anglo-Dutch War after he had been restored to the English throne, it's safe to say that Charles II was a lover, not a fighter. But, ladies, what a lover! His conquests included a couple of duchesses, a viscountess, an actress, a comedienne, Cardinal Mazarin's niece and his own wife's maid of honour. Unsurprisingly, Restoration England was littered with illegitimate blue-blooded sprogs sporting long curly hair and jaunty moustaches. Ironically, Charles never managed to get his own wife pregnant. He was probably too tired.

James II

Only good Catholic girls need apply for this one. Because of his almost pathological desire to Catholicise England, James turned an entire kingdom against himself. His nephew, the Duke of Monmouth, rebelled. James crushed the rebellion and ordered his nephew's head cut off. In one of the most famously botched executions in English history it took between five and eleven strokes to do the deed. Not cool. Protestant nobility invited James' sister to rule in his stead. James' army then refused to fight for him and he fled the country and never came back. Definitely not cool. Frankly, it's embarrassing.

William III

There is so much more to this staunchly Protestant Dutch monarch than the man who gave his name to a Northern Irish rambling society. Invited to England to rule in place of James II, William founded the Bank of England, accepted the Bill of Rights that ceded greater powers to Parliament and won a great Protestant victory against James at the Battle of the Boyne. For those looking for husband material, he was pretty progressive, leaving his wife Mary to rule the country in his stead while he clobbered Catholic France. However, his death was rather absurd: William died when he broke his collarbone after his horse tripped over a molehill. I'll bet it was a Catholic mole.

Bed

AT ONE POINT the nineteenth-century burglar Charles Frederick Peace was the most wanted man in Victorian England, having publically shot and killed a married love rival. On the run from the law, Charles Peace hid out in Nottingham. He holed up in seedy lodging house and soon became sexually involved with Susan Gray, a fellow resident.

The police combed Nottingham for the murderer/thief. It was believed that the police searched the lodging house where the murderer was resident and walked in on Peace and Gray while they were in bed together. Two factors saved Peace from arrest: a) the police had not yet twigged that the naked man beneath the sheets was Charles Peace, and b) these were eminently Victorian policeman, so there was certainly no 'Get your trousers on, you're nicked' from these sexually repressed coppers. Peace asked the embarrassed police officers if they wouldn't mind popping out while he got changed. The coppers obliged, whereupon Charles Peace leapt out of the window and escaped. Peace fled to London, taking Susan Gray with him.

Charles Peace was married all the time he was shooting other people's husbands and consorting with loose women; sometimes he even involved his wife in his strange sexual escapades. Anybody visiting Peace in London would have been greeted by a disguised outlaw and his wife (who was actually Susan Gray passing herself off as his wife) and would have been served tea and cakes by their housekeeper (who was, in fact, Charles Peace's actual wife Hannah). Both wife and mistress would eventually collude to betray Charles Peace to the authorities for money.

Now that's what I call *Upstairs, Downstairs*.

Three **KINGS** Called **GEORGE**

George I

George II

George III

  Choose one to bed, one to wed and one to behead!

George I

If you want good conversation on your date, unless you can speak French or German, George might not be the monarch for you. The first Hanoverian King of England never did bother to learn the language. Also, George was a strict stickler for fidelity in his women and took even perceived betrayal very seriously. George imprisoned his wife Sophia for an alleged affair with a Swedish count, locking her up in Ahlden House in Germany for over thirty years, leaving George free to do the nasty with his own mistress Melusine von der Schulenburg. What a name! Imagine fitting that on a valentine's card.

George II

In his time George crushed the Jacobite rebellion of 1745, and at Dettingen was the last King of England ever to lead his troops into battle. George was arrested and imprisoned by his own father but kicked his own son out of St James' Palace. George liked women. When George's dying wife told him to remarry, George replied, 'No, I will have mistresses.' Truth is, he'd already had mistresses – and told his wife about them. George was proper rock 'n' roll. And, like Elvis, he died on the toilet.

George III

George loved his wife Charlotte and never cheated on her. He pretty much built Buckingham Palace for her. But don't expect romantic getaways to the United States, as George was largely blamed for losing America in the War of Independence. Still, there would be plenty to do at home – like reading. George owned at least 65,000 books. Marriage to George would be long and prosperous and happy. Apart from the last ten years. That's when George went properly, clinically bonkers. One time he talked gibberish nonstop for two days. But if that's a definition of madness, then we're all mad, aren't we⸮

One Final **GEORGE**, a **WILLIAM** and a Controversial **ERNEST**

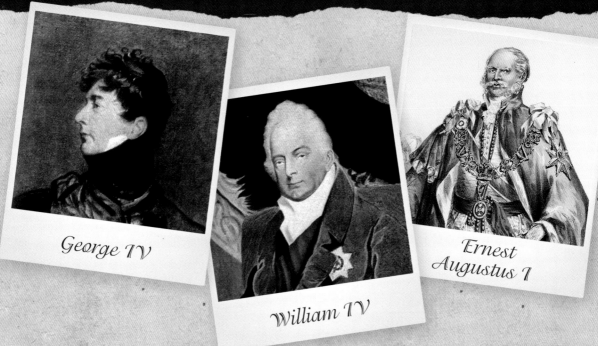

George IV

William IV

Ernest Augustus I

  Choose one to bed, one to wed and one to behead!

George IV

Prince Regent and eventual King of England, George IV was BIG in every sense of the word. He was a BIG spender, accruing massive debts and forking out £31,000 a year in stable costs alone. He was a BIG eater, weighing in excess of 20 stone. George was a BIG traditionalist, perpetuating the family custom of hating his father and being hated by his own subjects. Finally, on the BIG scale, having secretly wed the Catholic Maria Fitzherbert and then going on to marry Caroline of Brunswick without bothering to get a divorce, George IV was a BIGamist.

William IV

Although best known for being the dull and rather forgettable elderly king who was on the throne of England when the working classes were granted the vote, William IV was really rather splendid as a youngster. Admiral Horatio Nelson was his mate, George Washington tried to kidnap him, he got shot through the coat observing the destruction of Antwerp whilst hanging off a church steeple and, best of all, he shacked up with an actress and sired ten children. Eventually he had to settle down, become king and ditch the actress. But until then, Gung and Ho!

Ernest Augustus I

Not really a looker. This son of George III, King of Hanover and uncle to Queen Victoria received a slash to the face, a mangled arm and a dodgy eye during the War of the First Coalition. But that was nothing compared to leathering he received at the hands of his servant Joseph Sellis, who sabre whipped the royal for either a) sleeping with Sellis' wife, b) sleeping with Joseph Sellis, or c) sleeping with his valet, Cornelius Neale. Sellis was later found with his throat cut because d) he killed himself or e) was murdered to cover up a) b) or c).

ARCHBISHOPS
of CANTERBURY

Thomas Becket

Thomas Cranmer

William Laud

  Choose one to bed, one to wed and one to behead!

Thomas Becket

This one-time medieval playboy became religious in a hurry the moment he was made archbishop. Although friendly with Henry II, Thomas was certainly no respecter of persons, disagreeing with the king on issues like the authority of secular courts over the clergy. Thomas fled England for France. So if Thomas asks you to go on a romantic trip across the Channel, say yes. If he asks you to return to England, say no, because Thomas would die in Canterbury Cathedral, murdered by four knights who stabbed him in the monastic cloister, which I'm told is very painful.

Thomas Cranmer

This Tudor archbishop served two kings and a queen. He helped Henry VIII divorce his first wife and marry his second. He was responsible for much of the Anglican liturgy and the Book of Common Prayer. But Thomas had an indecisive side. When Mary I imprisoned him for treason, she demanded he recant his beliefs. Thomas recanted and then renounced his recantation four times before being burned alive, showing a refreshingly modern aspect of his personality. Who said it was only a woman's prerogative to change her mind?

William Laud

If you're a Puritan, don't even bother with this one. William hates you. He would replace that modest wooden communion table in your simply adorned place of worship with a nice stone altar. If you're a Scottish Puritan he would have forced you to use the English Prayer Book. If you challenged him, don't expect him to turn the other cheek: this crazy Christian would have had your ears sliced off (the fate of three unlucky and outspoken Puritans who criticised him in print). But William reaped what he sowed: he was executed by Puritans in the Civil War. So choose behead. William won't care. Been there, done that.

TUDOR and JACOBEAN PLAYWRIGHTS

William Shakespeare

Christopher Marlowe

Ben Jonson

  Choose one to bed, one to wed and one to behead!

William Shakespeare

William Shakespeare was a devout Catholic and a staunch Protestant. He was also an occultist. Shakespeare served in the army abroad, and never left the country. He was a faithful and adulterous husband and a devoted and negligent father. He was highly learned and poorly educated, a naturally intuitive genius incapable of being educated enough to write anything that clever. Shakespeare wrote the greatest plays in the English language without ever having actually written a single one. Shakespeare wasn't very funny. That's the one thing everybody agrees on.

Christopher Marlowe

This outstanding Tudor playwright was also a famous atheist. Anybody who considered sharing a flat with Marlowe ought to have been advised that Marlowe could also be a messy pup. He was always leaving things lying around the place – like atheistic pamphlets. When Marlowe's apartment was searched by the authorities his flatmate, Thomas Kyd, was arrested and tortured precisely because Marlowe didn't do his fair share of the tidying up. Marlowe was also something of a cheap date: he was stabbed to death in a seedy pub in Deptford after an argument over the bill – or alternatively, because he was an atheist, or a spy, or gay. It was one of those four. Probably.

Ben Jonson

Despite writing many comedies, Ben Jonson was the original angry young man of English theatre. In his time, Ben Jonson killed an actor in a duel, was imprisoned and branded for heresy, slagged off his contemporaries in numerous plays and was a suspect in the Gunpowder Plot. Ben Jonson was angry – really angry. You wouldn't have liked him when he was angry. In fact, you wouldn't have liked him when he wasn't angry. But that's difficult to determine, because he was always angry.

PRIVATEERS

Richard Grenville

Francis Drake

Walter Raleigh

  Choose one to bed, one to wed and one to behead!

Richard Grenville

If extreme violence turns you on, then vote Grenville. A date with Grenville is likely to involve him drinking a glass of wine, then biting into and chewing broken glass. If anyone hassles you, Grenville will sort them out – he never backed down from a fight. Grenville singlehandedly took on fifty-three Spanish warships, damaging sixteen of them before he was mortally wounded. On his deathbed Grenville called his own men 'traitors and dogs' for not fighting to the death. So, if you're the type of date who, before a fight, says, 'Leave it, Richard – they're not worth it', Richard will despise you.

Francis Drake

This great maritime Tudor overachiever did it all: he burned the port of Cadiz. He was the first Englishman to circumnavigate the globe. He trounced the Spanish Armada. But there is a more sensitive side to Drake; he was a devout Puritan. So a trip on a ship with Drake would involve attending two religious services a day.

Drake also loved music. On his voyage round the world he brought with him a company of viol and trumpet-playing musicians. So not only was Drake England's greatest explorer, he was also the nation's first rock band tour promoter.

Walter Raleigh

What a Renaissance man, what a Renaissance man, what a mighty good Renaissance man! Walter was an explorer, soldier, historian, poet and lover. Walter was good looking and walked with a rather sexy limp, due to a war wound. If you want to go on trip to the Tower of London, then choose Walter. He knows every inch of the place and will get you in for free. That's probably because he spent well over a decade there, locked up for antagonising Elizabeth I and James I, the latter eventually ordering Walter's execution.

MAD MEN and VISIONARIES

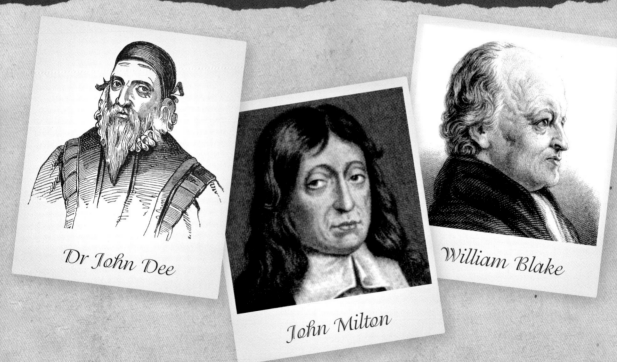

Dr John Dee

John Milton

William Blake

  Choose one to bed, one to wed and one to behead!

Dr John Dee

This Tudor astrologer was thought to have been Shakespeare's inspiration for the sorcerer Prospero in *The Tempest*. He certainly looked the part, with his long gown and wizardy beard. Dee believed that science (specifically mathematics) and magic were not mutually exclusive. He also believed that he could contact angels through reflective surfaces called 'scryer'. Once contacted, the angels would then dictate to Dee all the books that he would go on to write. That doesn't sound very traditionally angelic. No annunciating, smiting or laying waste to cities? Hark the herald angels-dictating-notes-to-a-beardy secretary – doesn't have the same ring to it, does it?

John Milton

Anyone considering a date with this radical, republican poet need be advised that he was blind at the peak of his creative powers. But don't worry about disability access when choosing venues for your date; Milton wouldn't leave his house. Perhaps it was because of all those anti-monarchy pamphlets he wrote just before Charles II was restored to the throne, making it safer to stay indoors. Never mind. But a nice evening in could be fun if you didn't mind acting as secretary and writing down all those endlessly long biblical epic poems Milton had rattling around in his head.

William Blake

England's weirdest visionary poet and painter was a very angry man and extremely difficult to get on with. Understandable, when you consider that he was once falsely accused of treason and never really sold any of his extraordinary works in his own lifetime. Blake also claimed to have been encouraged to write by archangels, observed angels in the trees in Peckham Rye and conversed with his dead brother. Mad? Probably. But the poet Wordsworth once said that he found Blake's madness more interesting than Byron's sanity. You could do worse. At least Blake isn't going to sleep with anything that moves.

ACTORS

Richard Burbage

Edmund Kean

Henry Irving

  Choose one to bed, one to wed and one to behead!

Richard Burbage

A true theatrical pioneer. Burbage was the first actor to play Hamlet, Richard III, King Lear and Othello. Burbage was Shakespeare's business partner. He built the famous Globe Theatre and built it in style, literally dismantling chunks of one theatre and moving it across the Thames as material for The Globe. Don't go on a date with this man to the theatre, though – especially to see him perform. The Globe burned down during a Burbage performance.

Edmund Kean

This outstanding tragedian of the late eighteenth and early nineteenth century revolutionised English stage acting by abandoning the popular declamatory style (or bad acting) and replacing it with a performance method more rooted in psychological realism. He also invented many of the modern clichés we associate with actors: megalomania, alcoholism, financial recklessness and nicking someone else's girlfriend. Kean was once successfully sued for adultery to the tune of £800. He also literally died on stage: cliché.

Henry Irving

As if Edmund Kean had never happened. Irving was a highly declamatory Victorian actor-manager deeply suspicious of the new, author-driven psychological dramas popular in freezing Northern Europe – so don't take him to see anything by Ibsen or Strindberg. But hanging out with Irving does mean you could visit the Lyceum Theatre for free, meet the actress Ellen Terry, or *Dracula* author Bram Stoker (who clerked for Irving). Some say Stoker based the character of Dracula on Irving. This makes sense. Irving was an intense presence who named himself after ghost-story writer Washington Irving. But the most compelling evidence for Irving as Dracula was that he drank blood, could turn into a bat and hated the playwright George Bernard Shaw. One of the above is true.

HIGHWAYMEN

Claude Duval

Dick Turpin

John Nevinson

Choose one to bed, one to wed and one to behead!

Claude Duval

Who'd have thought that the most genuinely gentlemanly of all English highwaymen would be French? Claude palled up with exiled Royalists, came to England during the Restoration of Charles II and then proceeded to rob the English on the highways of his adopted country. And the English loved him for it. Why wouldn't they? Claude looked gorgeous, dressed like a fashionista and loved to jig. He once gave money back to a victim whose wife agreed to dance with him by the roadside. How's that for a discount?

Dick Turpin

Do you smell something? Don't believe anything this highwayman tells you. He's full of it. If Dick promises to take you for a horse ride on his legendary steed Black Bess, he's lying: Black Bess was completely invented by the writer William Harrison Ainsworth. If Dick regales you with stories of his epic dash on horseback from Kent to York, he's lying. Someone else did it. Dick wasn't even from Yorkshire. He was an Essex boy. And if Dick ever offers to defend your honour, he'll cock it up – Dick accidentally shot his own friend dead while trying to rescue him. In conclusion, when all is said and done, our Dick is a bit of a …

John Nevinson

The outlaw who actually made the London to York run, probably. Nevinson was the genuine article. Nevinson was well mannered and principled in his crimes, robbing only those who could afford it. He abhorred violence (except in the case of that nightwatchman he was accused of murdering – but we're all allowed one slip up, aren't we?). Nevinson was the perfect gentleman and a guaranteed excellent date – unless you like horses. Nevinson would occasionally kill a horse for fear he might be identified by his mount. Nevinson knew horses couldn't talk, didn't he?

ARCHITECTS

Inigo Jones

Christopher Wren

Sir John Soane

  who would you bed, wed, behead?

Inigo Jones

What a great name! Inigo was the first architect to introduce Renaissance designs in Britain. He started out designing the costumes and scenery for royal entertainments, which led to his post as Surveyor-General of the King's Works. Inigo built the banqueting house at Whitehall Palace and the New Exchange in the Strand. So if you want a nice house, marry Inigo. But Inigo was an architect closely associated with royal commissions. So if you're interested, make sure you make your move before the start of the English Civil War. Offers of work seemed to dry up for Inigo after 1642.

Christopher Wren

Wren was Professor of Astronomy at both Gresham College and Oxford and he helped found the Royal Society. Oh yes, and he designed a new St Paul's Cathedral after the original burned down during the Great Fire of London. Wren was also something of a whiz at maths, probably a freemason and, as a child, invented a contraption that could write in the dark. That's much more impressive than building a massive church that's never open when I visit it and costs too much to get in.

Sir John Soane

If you don't like going out, this Egyptophile and expert in neoclassical architecture could be your man. Why leave the house when you can live in John Soane's famous museum, hang out in a pharaoh's coffin and entertain dinner guests like J.M.W. Turner and Samuel Taylor Coleridge? Soane is a devoted husband – but for Anubis' sake, don't have kids! Your son will shame the family when he knocks up his sister-in-law. But you can take solace in your husband's lasting legacy: a sarcophagus Soane designed formed the basis for the traditional English phone box. Remember them? Proper phones? For the love of Osiris! It wasn't that long ago!

Bed

TUDOR SOLDIER, EXPLORER, POET and historian: Walter Raleigh's technique as a lover was so skilful that he could completely discombobulate a woman's speech patterns without even lying down. The seventeenth-century biographical sketch writer John Aubrey relayed this anecdote about Raleigh:

> He loved a wench well; and one time getting one of the maids of honour up against a tree in a wood (it was his first lady) who seemed at first boarding to be something fearful of her honour, and modest, she cried, 'Sweet Sir Walter, what do you me ask? Will you undo me? Nay, sweet Sir Walter! Sweet Sir Walter! Sir Walter!' At last, as the danger and the pleasure at the same time grew higher, she cried in the ecstasy, 'Swisser Swatter, Swisser Swatter!'

Narrowly avoiding disaster in this fashion was pure Tudor Viagra to Raleigh, and for ten years he played the field in like fashion. But the irony of Walter's love life was that it was marriage that got him into trouble. Raleigh fell in love with Elizabeth Throckmorton, an attractive and highly intelligent woman. She served at Court as Lady of the Privy Chamber to Queen Elizabeth I. Throckmorton fell pregnant by Raleigh and the two married in secret. As an intimate servant to Elizabeth I, Throckmorton could not marry without her queen's permission. When the queen finally found out, she was furious and imprisoned the rebellious couple in the Tower of London. Raleigh was released first, but Elizabeth was forced to remain incarcerated for short while longer. Consequently, Raleigh's immediate predicament gave rise to an idiom commonly used to this day by Englishmen to describe their wives: 'Her indoors.'

VERA EFFIGIES CLARISS^{mi} VIRI Dⁿⁱ GUALTHERI RALEGH EQ. AUR.

PRIME MINISTERS

Robert Walpole

William Pitt
(the Elder)

William Pitt
(the Younger)

  Choose one to bed, one to wed and one to behead!

Robert Walpole

If maths geeks turn you on, then Walpole is probably the man for you. Walpole was the very first prime minister who, in 1720, when the South Sea Company collapsed, saved England from financial ruin. But if you are going on a date with Walpole, best avoid the theatre, especially if *The Beggar's Opera* is in town. It contains a character called Peachum, who is a criminal and dispenser of bribes believed to be based on Walpole. Was Walpole really a criminal and dispenser of bribes? Well, I wouldn't let him anywhere near my end-of-year accounts.

William Pitt (the Elder)

The most beloved of all eighteenth-century prime ministers, Pitt the Elder was awesome. As Secretary of State he steered the country to victory in the Seven Years' War and helped establish Britain's empire. A proper man of the people, William was called 'The Great Commoner' by his fans. In fact, in the name of a good cause, he would take on anybody, including the king and Robert Walpole. What's not to love? Well, William could be very sarcastic. He was even dismissed from the army for being too sarcastic. So if William tells you that you 'look nice in that dress', you don't.

William Pitt (the Younger)

What a prodigy. Graduated from Cambridge at 17. MP at 21. Prime minister at 24. And that's before he got started. In his day, young Pitt curtailed the power of the mighty East India Company, united Ireland under the Act of Union and steered England to victory against the French in the early stages of the Napoleonic Wars. Impressed? Well, he did also introduce income tax. And no one likes a try-hard, do they? I bet he was no good at PE.

ROMANTIC POETS

William Wordsworth

John Keats

Lord Byron

  Choose one to bed, one to wed and one to behead!

William Wordsworth

This former Poet Laureate pretty much kick-started the Romantic Movement. Wordsworth loved nature and emotion in equal measure. Dates with Wordsworth would consist of long, silent walks in the country getting misty-eyed over billowing clouds. If that makes Wordsworth sound oh-so-sensitive, beware. Wordsworth's politics revealed a darker side. For a while, our Will was a big fan of Napoleon Bonaparte. Thankfully this didn't last: Will became disillusioned with Bonaparte when he realised that his hero was actually a tyrannical megalomaniac. Amazing! These poets percieve things we mere mortals simply cannot comprehend.

John Keats

If suffering artists turn you on, then John Keats is definitely the man for you. Keats' mum died of tuberculosis. His dad was killed by a horse. Keats' inheritance money was never released to him and he remained poor all his life. Poverty kept Keats from marrying the woman he loved and despite being lauded by Shelley (who died in possession of a book of his poems), Keats' verse was largely ignored in his lifetime. Keats died, aged 25, of TB in Italy. Could have been worse: Anne Brontë died of TB in Scarborough. At least the weather was nice.

Lord Byron

The dark lord of English Romantic poetry. This howling mad poet and political radical drank wine from a human skull, almost certainly knocked up his half-sister Augusta, was hounded out of England, was present in Geneva when Mary Shelley wrote *Frankenstein*, knocked up her step-sister Claire Claremont and died of fever on the way to liberate Greece from their Ottoman oppressors. Did I mention that Byron almost certainly knocked up his half-sister Augusta? So, unless you're a blood relative, best not to bother with this one. What am I saying? I just partially justified incest.

REFORMERS

William Wilberforce

John Wesley

John Howard

  Choose one to bed, one to wed and one to behead!

William Wilberforce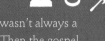

This Member of Parliament for Hull is most famous for ending the British slave trade. But he wasn't always a goody-two-shoes: as a student at Cambridge, young Wilberforce was quite the party animal. Then the gospel came-a-calling and Wilberforce cleaned up his act and devoted his life to numerous social causes such as education, the suppression of vice and, of course, the abolition of slavery. That's all well and good, but was he FIT? Apparently he was. And quite a smooth talker. So, if you want your date full of yummy moral goodness wrapped in a beefy package, then use the Wilberforce.

John Wesley

This obsessive diarist and founder of the Methodist denomination of Christianity certainly liked to travel. So, if you want to see England, Wesley's your man. Riding around the country on horseback preaching his message of holiness, Wesley could attract crowds of up to 20,000 people. But Wesley's sermons often ended in massive riots, as members of the crowd sought to kill him. Despite being exceedingly moral, Wesley was not necessarily marriage material. He famously hated his wife and didn't even attend her funeral. That's probably why he travelled so much. Anything to get out of the house.

John Howard

This filthy-rich Christian used his wealth to fund a campaign to improve the appalling prison conditions in Georgian England. Howard obsessively travelled around the country visiting most of the nation's gaols. He did the same in Europe, clocking up 49,000 miles over fifteen years of trips to the Continent. So, life with Howard would mean a life on the road, if that appeals to you. However, Howard's life of travel could also be dangerous as he visited many squalid and disease-ridden institutions. It's amazing he didn't catch anything. Oops, my mistake. He did. In 1790, Howard contracted typhus in the Ukraine and died.

SCIENTISTS

Isaac Newton

Charles Babbage

Charles Darwin

  Choose one to bed, one to wed and one to behead!

Isaac Newton

It's a common misconception that Newton invented gravity. He didn't. He just pointed it out to those who hadn't noticed it before and then took all the credit. But ladies, there's more to Newton than the basic principles of 'what goes up must come down'. Newton was a college dropout (admittedly because of the plague of 1665, and he did go back in '67). He suffered from depression, was divisive, paranoid, pathologically guilty and liked to argue. He was an MP and became Warden of the Royal Mint. I love mints, but I've never had a royal one.

Charles Babbage

A great advert for home education. Ill health kept young Charles away from school. That didn't stop him getting into Cambridge and going on to design the Difference and Analytical Engine. The what? That's the first ever computer to you and me, although it was basically a massive calculator that that looked like a giant knitting machine. If clever appeals to you, then you will be royally turned on to know that when Babbage died his brain was removed, cut in half and displayed in two museums. So, don't choose behead. What would be the point?

Charles Darwin

We all know that Darwin wrote *On the Origin of Species* and formulated the theory of evolution, but was he any fun to hang out with? Not really. All that writing about monkeys and mutations induced a mysterious illness that caused him to vomit, shake, and sprout boils whenever he found himself in a social situation. He wasn't very romantic either. When weighing up the pros and cons of whether to marry his cousin Emma (the obvious con being 'she's your cousin'), a tick in the plus column was that she was 'better than a dog'.

William Lamb
aka Lord Melbourne

William Gladstone

Benjamin
Disraeli

 Choose one to bed, one to wed and one to behead!

William Lamb aka Lord Melbourne

If you want to go to London and visit the queen, then why not give Melbourne a try? Melbourne was the prime minister most beloved of Queen Victoria, who regarded him as something of a father figure. But if you are a bit on the common side, then don't bother. Melbourne didn't like poor people and didn't think that they should vote. Even if you pass the posh test, beware. Don't read poetry to Melbourne, hoping to get him in the mood. His wife once got it on with Lord Byron, and ever since, 'Childe Harold's Pilgrimage' has always been something of a passion killer.

William Gladstone

If you want to go to London and visit the queen, then give Gladstone a wide birth. Queen Victoria hated him, calling him a 'mad old firebrand'. But he was alright. He cleaned up the justice system and reformed education and the civil service. But he will be best remembered as the PM who failed to save the marooned maverick general Charles Gordon when he was stranded in Khartoum. Gladstone's nickname used to be GOM = 'Grand Old Man'. When Gordon was killed it became MOG = 'Murderer of Gordon'. OMG. LOL.

Benjamin Disraeli

Disraeli is the classic case of 'if at first you don't succeed, try, try again'. Disraeli failed at business, got into massive debt, went mad for a bit and was knocked back four times before finally being elected MP for Maidstone. So if you choose Disraeli, know that he will not quit on you. If that sounds a bit too intense, be encouraged that Disraeli had a lighter side. He wrote novels – lots of novels. So despite a political legacy that improved health, protected unions and secured British financial interests in the Suez Canal, Disraeli's lasting legacy was setting a precedent for politicians everywhere to think they can write novels – lots of novels. Thanks, Diz. Behead!

ENGINEERS

Robert Stephenson

Isambard
Kingdom Brunel

Thomas Bouch

  Choose one to bed, one to wed and one to behead!

Robert Stephenson

Do you have a need for speed? Then choose Robert. This Geordie engineer invented the first steam engine. On its initial trials, Stephenson's train achieved a top speed of 29mph. Steady on!

Stevenson famously called his train the *Rocket*. But Stephenson designed another train: The *Lancashire Witch* (a much better name, in my opinion). I wasn't being sarcastic when I put out the call for adrenaline junkies at the beginning of this profile. Hanging out with Stephenson could be dangerous. On one of its early runs, Stephenson's *Rocket* accidentally killed a Member of Parliament.

Isambard Kingdom Brunel

He built the Clifton Suspension Bridge, the steamship SS *Great Britain* and most of the bridges, viaducts and tunnels for the Great Western Railway. Brunel was the greatest British engineer of the lot. Except he wasn't. His dad was French, making Brunel half-French. Besides, he wasn't all that clever. Brunel once performed a magic trick for his children that went wrong, leaving a coin lodged in his throat. He couldn't engineer his way out of that embarrassing predicament and had to be turned upside down until the coin was dislodged. *Vive la Révolution Industrielle!*

Thomas Bouch

Never heard of him? Bouch invented the world's first roll-on roll-off ferry service for trains. But that's not the real reason he's famous. Bouch built the Tay Bridge, using girders which nobody used quite like Thomas Bouch. He was knighted for his work on the Tay Bridge. But that's not the real reason he's famous. The Tay Bridge collapsed within a year of Bouch having built it, killing seventy-five people. That's why he's famous. Bouch died shortly after his appalling blunder, and the Tay Bridge was completed by William Arrol. Date him instead. He built Tower Bridge. As far as I'm aware, that's still standing.

ENGLISHMEN
Who Went NATIVE

William Adams

James Hudson Taylor

T.E. Lawrence

  Choose one to bed, one to wed and one to behead!

William Adams

Also known as Anjin Miura, Gillingham-born William Adams was thought to have been the first Englishman to visit Japan and was certainly the first to be granted samurai status. Originally with the Dutch East India Company, William became trade advisor, diplomat and a favourite of the Shogun Tokugawa Ieyasu. The Shogun liked Adams well enough to give him the gift of two swords but didn't like him enough to let him return to England and retrieve his family. So if you choose wed and William is late home from work, don't wait up for him.

James Hudson Taylor

This missionary and founder of the non-denominational China Inland Mission spent fifty-one years in China, could speak in many local dialects, wore Chinese clothing and adopted a Chinese orphan as his own child. Hudson also took on the opium trade and lived through some of the most violent periods of nineteenth-century Chinese history, during which many fellow missionaries were killed. Ladies, this man was brave. He was also well prepared: prior to leaving England for China, Hudson Taylor trained for any prospective hardship by spending time in Hull. I'll bet surviving the Boxer Rebellion was a breeze after that.

T. E. Lawrence

On an archaeological expedition in Palestine, Thomas Edward Lawrence fell in love with Arabia, learned Arabic and became an Arab nationalist. By the end of the First World War Lawrence was a hero, dressing in Arab clothing and leading guerrilla attacks on the Turkish forces culminating in his famous assault on the city of Aqaba. Tempted, ladies? But wasn't Lawrence gay? In all probability, no. But he was a masochist. So what's the key to dating Lawrence? Well, they say the way to a man's heart is through his stomach. Punch Lawrence in the stomach. He'd like that. Then give him six of the best.

HEROES

Horatio Nelson

James Cook

Robert Falcon Scott

  Choose one to bed, one to wed and one to behead!

Horatio Nelson

This hero of Trafalgar was more man with one eye and a missing arm than most physically intact males are ever likely to be. Yet he was horribly seasick. So don't take him boating on your first date. Also, a 3D film is off the cards. Nelson gave good quote in the heat of battle. Before Trafalgar, Nelson inspired his men, declaiming 'England expects every man to do his duty'. His last words were 'God and Country'. But he also said 'Westminster Abbey! or glorious victory!' before the battle of Cape St Vincent, which is, quite frankly, crap.

James Cook

This Yorkshire man, Whitby resident and discoverer of Australia was a good catch. Cook was tall and handsome, with striking brown eyes. He was self-effacing and shy, but a spirited conversationalist. Marry him but don't have kids. Half of them died horribly. The other half had no children of their own, thus permanently extinguishing Cook's hereditary line. Cook's own demise was pretty gruesome. He was clubbed to the ground by Hawaiians and stabbed to death. But other, friendlier Hawaiians claimed his skeleton and used it in their sacred ceremonial rites. Are you Hawaiian yourself? Then choose the captain. You can always brag that you jumped Cook's bones.

Robert Falcon Scott

We Brits love a good tale of heroic failure laced with irony. Scott famously failed to beat the Norwegians to the South Pole and then froze to death on the way back, expiring a mere 20 kilometres away from food and supplies. And we love Scott for doing it, or not doing it. Who remembers the name of the Norwegians who beat Scott to the punch anyway, apart from the Norwegians, who like winning? But we hate winning and we hate winners. The first shall be last and every loser wins. So choose Scott. You great big loser. We love you.

AUTHORS

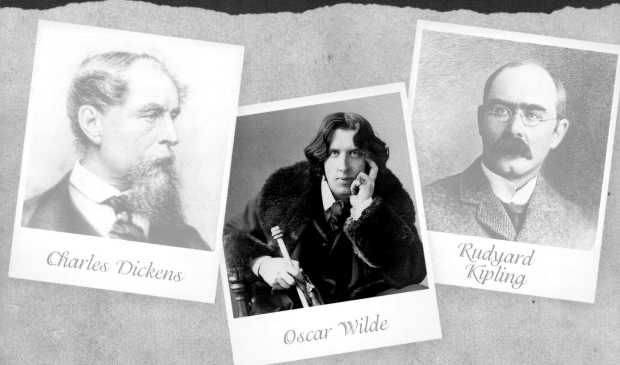

Charles Dickens

Oscar Wilde

Rudyard Kipling

  Choose one to bed, one to wed and one to behead!

Charles Dickens

You might think it fun to date the world's most famous novelist. But do you really want to end up as a figure of fear, pathos or derision in one of his books? Bill Sykes, Little Nell, Mrs Nickleby and Inspector Bucket were all based on neighbours, relatives and associates. Dickens even put his chiropodist in *David Copperfield*. And with the line so blurred between the real and the fictitious, Dickens will inevitably confuse you with someone else, having once posted his wife a gift originally intended for his mistress. But he's a genius, so that kind of behaviour is perfectly justifiable.

Oscar Wilde

This luminous Anglo-Irish playwright, novelist, poet, convict, proto-gay rights activist and wit would certainly be a fun date – if you can stand the constant barrage of one liners. 'I have nothing to declare but my genius.' That was him. 'Always forgive your enemies, nothing annoys them so much.' That was one of his. 'Either the wallpaper goes or I do.' He might have said that. 'A handbag!?!' He definitely wrote that. Hilarious! Oh, you think so? Well, humour's a very subjective thing.

Rudyard Kipling

This novelist and journalist literally wrote like a madman. A date with Kipling would most likely involve him arriving spattered with ink. Considering marriage? You will never be Kipling's first concern. Kipling called the *Civil and Military Gazette* his 'mistress and true love'. Kipling wrote a lot about India and Empire. Consequently, George Orwell thought that Kipling was a tool and accused him of being an imperialist. But Kipling was the first Englishman to win the Nobel Prize for Literature, so that's probably just the jealousy talking. Besides, Kipling wrote *The Jungle Book*, so he can do no wrong. He wrote the words but not the music. On second thoughts, perhaps George Orwell was right.

EXPLORERS

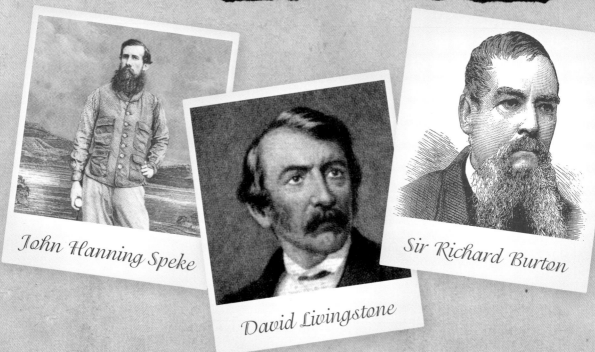

John Hanning Speke

David Livingstone

Sir Richard Burton

  Choose one to bed, one to wed and one to behead!

John Hanning Speke

This soldier, explorer and discoverer of Lake Victoria was a real Victorian man's man, ladies. Speke once cut a beetle out of his ear with a knife and escaped from Somali tribesmen with a spear sticking out of his hip. Like all great men's men, Speke wasn't very good at spelling and believed all animals existed for the purpose of target practice. Speke feared nothing, with the exception of public speaking. That really gave him the willies. So much so that he shot himself dead before a public debate at the Royal Society. Manly!

David Livingstone

A date with this Scottish evangelical medical missionary would never be bereft of interesting anecdotes, like the time he discovered Victoria Falls, walked across Africa, was attacked by a lion, or dismantled the African slave trade. If you're concerned about Livingstone preaching at you, don't worry: he was rubbish at it. He only converted one African, who still refused to renounce his polygamist ways. If you're considering marriage, don't expect Livingstone to stick around. Livingstone's wife didn't see him for years at a stretch, became an alcoholic and died of malaria.

Sir Richard Burton

Not the Welsh actor. This Richard Burton's much better than that. He could speak around thirty languages, was an outstanding swordsman and walked to Mecca disguised as a dervish. Burton had the most striking face of any Victorian, bearing a sexy scar from when a Somali tribesman shoved a spear through his chops. But there were scandals and rumours. He translated the *Kama Sutra* into English and was said to have committed murder in Arabia and frequent homosexual brothels in India. Bed, wed and behead. He'd probably enjoy all three.

Wed

THE FILM STAR and hedonist Errol Flynn once put a dead snake in the undergarments of his favourite co-star Olivia de Havilland as a practical joke. Why? Some believe it was Flynn's arrested way of telling de Havilland he loved her, because he was too emotionally stunted to actually *tell* her he loved her.

A similar psychology could be attributed to John Wilmot, the great Restoration rake, poet and writer of pornographic verse. Wilmot clearly had no trouble bedding women he cared very little about. But when it came to wooing the young aristocrat Elizabeth Mallet, a spectacular display of misdirected affection was called for. Wilmot gathered together a group of armed adventurers and had them kidnap Elizabeth at Charing Cross. Elizabeth was transferring from her own coach into an adjoining carriage to be spirited away to Wilmot. The plan went wrong. Wilmot was arrested and was placed in the Tower of London until he formally apologised to none other than Charles II, whom the incident had personally offended.

Unsurprisingly, Errol Flynn and Olivia de Havilland never got together. Surprisingly, John Wilmot and Elizabeth Mallet *did* get together. Despite the attentions of numerous wealthier and far more eligible suitors, Elizabeth eventually succumbed to Wilmot's attentions. John and Elizabeth ran away and were married in secret in a chapel in Knightsbridge. The marriage lasted all of John Wilmot's life and was characterised by a strong and unconditional love, i.e. Wilmot carried on whoring, secure in the knowledge that Elizabeth would always take him back. It is strongly believed that John Wilmot died of a combination of multiple venereal infections combined with massive alcohol abuse. He was 33 years old.

Olivia de Havilland, we salute you.

NORMAN QUEENS
and CONSORTS

Matilda of Flanders

Matilda of Scotland

Adeliza of Louvain

  Choose one to bed, one to wed and one to behead!

Matilda of Flanders

If you're one of those sensitive 'new man' types and want to date the diminutive (she was as little as 4ft 2in) wife of William the Conqueror, forget about it. Both literally and figuratively, Matilda liked to date bastards. Husband William was of dubious parentage. He was also reputed to have pulled Matilda off her horse by her hair and dragged her through the streets when she initially refused his proposal of marriage. Her response? She refused to marry anyone else. So, hardly a poster girl for feminism then. Rest assured, if you don't behead her, then Germaine Greer certainly will.

Matilda of Scotland

A truly blessed match if all that stuff in the Bible about peacemakers being blessed is true. This virtuous Scottish lovely held England together with her beatific gorgeousness during the reign of her husband Henry I. Matilda's marriage unified two warring royal dynastic lines. Matilda arbitrated in a disagreement between Henry and a prominent archbishop. On top of that, she washed poor people's feet and founded a couple of leper colonies. She was known as 'the Good Queen' and 'Matilda of the Blessed Memory'. Another nickname was 'Godiva'. So, at least behind closed doors, you can bet Matilda was pretty filthy.

Adeliza of Louvain

This poetry-loving Belgian beauty came from good stock (she was related to Charlemagne) and owned all of Chichester as well as a large chunk of London. Adeliza travelled everywhere with her king and husband Henry I, and spent the majority of her spare time trying to produce a legitimate heir to the English throne. This was not as erotic as it sounds. When the couple married, Henry was in his 50s. Adeliza was in her teens. She (unsurprisingly) failed to conceive. But when Henry died, Adeliza remarried and had seven children with the more age-appropriate Earl of Arundel. Go figure.

More **NORMAN QUEENS** and **CONSORTS**

Matilda of Boulogne

Berengaria of Navarre

Isabella of Angoulême

  Choose one to bed, one to wed and one to behead!

Matilda of Boulogne

During the war between King Stephen and Empress Matilda, Stephen's wife, Matilda of Boulogne, dropped a sprog and immediately sailed across the English Channel to assist her husband. When the war went badly for Stephen, Queen Matilda besieged Dover Castle, lifted the Siege of Winchester, negotiated a treaty with Scotland and booted Empress Matilda out of London. So, if you're looking for the medieval equivalent of the type of 'Don't mess with my man' kind of girl that would follow a rival female into the ladies' toilet at a nightclub and hit them in the head with their high-heeled shoe, look no further.

Berengaria of Navarre

Fancy going to the Holy Land for a honeymoon/busman's holiday? Choose Berengaria. This Spanish princess pursued Richard I whilst he was on his way to retake Jerusalem from the Saracens, but was captured en route and imprisoned in Cyprus. Richard heard about it, invaded Cyprus and married Berengaria on the spot. Romantic gesture? Probably not. Richard just liked killing people. But when Richard died, Berengaria mourned hard. Genuine grief? Probably not. More likely a lament of not getting any bedroom action as a consequence of marrying an extremely fit but secretly gay king.

Isabella of Angoulême

King John's second wife was more than a match for the unpopular King of England in terms of unpleasant behaviour, but got away with it because she was fantastically fit. Isabella was bad tempered. It didn't matter. She was fit. Her subjects likened her to the Emperor Caligula's evil wife. So what? She was fit. After John's death, Isabella married her own daughter's fiancé. Who cares! Fit! Isabella was suspected of trying to poison the King of France. Completely forgiven. Why? Fit! Fit! Fit! Actually that last example is somewhat inaccurate. The French king tried to arrest her but she escaped. How? Sheer physical fitness!

SHE–WOLVES of ENGLAND

Matilda

Eleanor of Aquitaine

Isabella

  Choose one to bed, one to wed and one to behead!

Matilda

When Henry I died, Matilda was the legitimate heir to the English throne until her grasping cousin Stephen usurped her title. But if you think you'll be dating a royal pushover, think again. Matilda didn't take this outrage lying down. She invaded England and imprisoned Stephen at Lincoln. But Matilda was arrogant, didn't rule well and forgot to get crowned, paving the way for Stephen to retake the throne. So don't call Matilda 'Queen' or 'Queenie'; she doesn't like it. But then Matilda was also wife to a Holy Roman Emperor and therefore an Empress, so what's she complaining about? Some people!

Eleanor of Aquitaine

This estranged wife of Henry II and mother of two kings (Richard I and John) was one of the most formidable ladies of the Middle Ages: ruling England as queen dowager when Richard was off fighting the Turks and supporting her sons when they rebelled against their father. Not one to be messed with then? But there was a softer side to Eleanor. Alongside her daughter, Eleanor ran something called the Court of Love, which was a sort of tribunal presiding over affairs of the heart. Imagine a medieval Judge Judy for simpering nincompoops. Something like that.

Isabella

Isabella was the long-suffering wife of a homosexual king and a usurping welsh regent. Called 'the She-Wolf of France', Isabella was married off at 12 to Edward II, who neglected her in favour of young noblemen. Consequently Isabella fell in love with the swashbuckling Celt Roger Mortimer, who helped her overthrow her husband. Isabella and Roger probably ordered Edward's gruesome murder, before ruling badly and being usurped by Isabella's teenage son. Isabella was spared. Mortimer wasn't. So don't even consider marriage unless you want to be hanged, drawn and quartered or have a cow horn rammed up your jacksie.

ROSES of the WARS of the ROSES

Elizabeth Woodville

Lady Margaret Beaufort

Anne Neville

  Choose one to bed, one to wed and one to behead!

Elizabeth Woodville

This beautiful noblewoman might have accidentally exacerbated the Wars of the Roses by marrying Edward IV for love, but my-oh-my, what excellent genes. Pretty much all of Elizabeth's children, grandchildren and great-grandchildren went on to achieve magnificence. Wed this one. Who knows what your kids are going to become. They could end up a king that creates the Church of England or a queen that defeats the Spanish Armada. Alternatively they might get murdered in the Tower of London or burn lots of Puritans alive. You pays your money and you takes your chance.

Lady Margaret Beaufort

When on a date with the mother of Henry VII, don't mention her exes. It's a touchy subject. Margaret was married off before her third birthday. The marriage was annulled. By the time Margaret was 13, she had married for the second time and had given birth to the future King of England. Her second and third husbands died. Fourth time lucky? Margaret persuaded her fourth husband to betray Richard III at the battle of Bosworth, paving the way for the Tudor dynasty. Choose bed by all means, but don't underestimate the power of pillow talk.

Anne Neville

As daughter of the mighty Earl of Warwick, Anne was used mercilessly as an alliance-cementing bargaining chip. Anne was married off to Edward VI's son. He died and Anne became ward of the Duke of Clarence and then wife to Richard III. Anne was passed around like the parmesan at an Italian restaurant. But, if you like the idea of wedding an easily manipulated wallflower, make sure you don't outlive her. When Anne died, there was an eclipse of the sun. This was interpreted as a portent of doom for Richard, who was suspected of poisoning her. And we all know what happened after that.

WIVES of HENRY VIII

Catherine of Aragon

Anne Boleyn

Jane Seymour

  Choose one to bed, one to wed and one to behead!

Catherine of Aragon

Blue eyed, flame haired and Spanish, Henry VIII's first wife made for a decent and happy marriage until she reached her forty-second birthday, failed to produce a male heir and was divorced, accidentally resculpting the religious landscape of Europe. Catherine combined the qualities of religious devotion and physical beauty, like few royals. It was thought that she was the model for Michael Sittow's portrait of Mary Magdalene. Religious philosopher Thomas More said that 'There were few women who could compete with the Queen in her prime', which is a polite Tudor euphemism for 'I'd do her'.

Anne Boleyn

This mysterious Tudor wild child who stirred the loins of a randy king, was, by many accounts, not actually that pretty. She may or may not have had an extra finger on one hand and had moles on her neck that constantly drew comments. But she had amazing eyes. Today you might call them 'come to bed eyes'. In the 1500s, they would have been called 'come to bed, divorce your wife, marry me, fall out with the Pope, cause a mighty religious schism, accuse me of adultery and incest and then chop my head off' eyes. Approach with caution.

Jane Seymour

Jane worked for both of Henry's VIII's previous wives, so when the king started giving her the eye, she must have felt more fear than flattery. Henry married Jane the day after he beheaded Anne Boleyn. If Jane had any misgivings, she kept them to herself. In fact, she didn't say much at all. This could have been born out of prudence, or the fact that Jane was a bit thick, being virtually illiterate. It didn't matter. Jane avoided divorce or execution and gave Henry the son he wanted. Unfortunately, Jane died as a consequence of complications in childbirth. Isn't it ironic? Don't you think?

More **WIVES** of **HENRY VIII**

Anne of Cleves

Catherine Howard

Catherine Parr

  Choose one to bed, one to wed and one to behead!

Anne of Cleves

A cautionary tale for anyone considering doctoring their dating profile picture: Henry VIII fell in love with this German royal on the strength of her likeness in a Holbein portrait. When Anne arrived in England, Henry was not happy with the result: he called Anne 'the mare of Flanders'. Henry married her anyway but had the wedding annulled six months later. Apparently, Henry never slept with Anne. Instead, he paid Anne off, moved her into his dead wife's father's house and gave Anne the honorific title the 'King's beloved sister'. What is wrong with these Tudors?

Catherine Howard

The music and animal-loving Catherine Howard was pretty, charming and fun-loving but not particularly bright. In fact, a date with Catherine might very likely accidentally result in you getting hanged, drawn and, let us not forget, quartered. By the time she married the old, bloated and physically ailing Henry VIII, Catherine was in love with her former House Secretary Francis Dereham. Catherine lived very much in the moment, lacking any sense of recent history and its consequences. Catherine employed Francis Dereham in the royal household and carried on seeing him. Henry found out. Guess what happened next?

Catherine Parr

Catherine was smart and devout. She was an expert in reform theology and the first queen of England to author books without having to use a pseudonym. Catherine was also the consummate survivor. Thrice widowed, she survived being taken hostage by rebels during the Pilgrimage of Grace; she survived attempts at court to blacken her name by anti-reformists and, most impressive of all, Catherine survived marriage to Henry VIII. Catherine outlived Henry, marrying her true love Thomas Seymour. If Gloria Gaynor was around back then, she would have written a song about Catherine Parr. But Catherine died in childbirth aged 36. So perhaps not.

TUDOR QUEENS

Lady Jane Grey

Mary I

Elizabeth I

  Choose one to bed, one to wed and one to behead!

Lady Jane Grey

Anyone thinking about dating or marrying Lady Jane Grey would have to contend with perhaps the pushiest parents in English history. Worse than any stage mum and dad, Protestant husband and wife Lady Frances Brandon and Henry Grey virtually forced their daughter on to the English throne in an attempt to stop the legitimate heir Mary Tudor Catholicising England. Jane lasted nine days before being imprisoned and then beheaded. To cap it all, her own dad denounced her before being imprisoned and then beheaded himself. Good! Serves him right!

Mary I

She may not have been one of history's great lookers, but Mary Tudor was guaranteed to keep you warm at night – if you were a Protestant, that is. Mary's enthusiasm for brutally immolating Puritans earned her the nickname 'Bloody Mary'. The name has been deemed unfair in recent years, as Mary only burned just under 300 Protestants – which was chickenfeed compared with the number of Catholics her sister Elizabeth executed during her reign. But I haven't burned any Protestants to death. Nor do I know anyone who has, which still makes Mary a bit of a psycho in my book. Best avoid.

Elizabeth I

Anybody considering going on a date with the greatest female monarch ever to sit on an English throne should bear in mind that they are highly unlikely to get anywhere near what is technically known as 'fourth base'. Elizabeth Tudor did not put out for anyone. In fact, Elizabeth I led on many of the greats of sixteenth-century Europe, including Phillip II of Spain and Henry Francis, the Duke of Anjou. She didn't handle rejection particularly well either, having gone to war with Phillip, exiled Sir Walter Raleigh and executed her thigh-slapping toy boy Robert Devereux, the Earl of Essex. As far as bedding or wedding Elizabeth was concerned, your best option would be to keep a safe distance and bask in her reflected glory. Alternatively, you could ask her cousin Mary out. She was well up for it.

Wed

HENRY FIELDING, the author of *Tom Jones* and founder of the Bow Street Runners, suffered much in the name of love. He was married twice. The first marriage was rocked by tragedy and the second by scandal. As a youth, an early failed attempt at marriage even earned him a good hiding.

In 1725, the young Fielding fell in love with wealthy Lyme Regis lass named Sarah Andrews. Fielding was relatively poor and out of the running, as far as Sarah's guardian Andrew Miller was concerned. Fielding pursued Sarah regardless.

Sitting in an inn, Fielding and his friends were attacked by a gang of thugs, strongly believed to have been hired by Miller. Fielding fought back and injured one of the thugs, and was hauled before the courts for assault. He then made one more attempt at winning Sarah's favour: he tried to kidnap her on the way to church. He failed, cut his losses and fled Lyme Regis.

In 1734, Fielding married Charlotte Craddock. The marriage lasted ten years before Charlotte died of fever. Fielding's daughter died the same year. In his grief, Henry Fielding was supported by his surviving daughter, his sister and Charlotte's maid Mary Daniels. Whatever support Mary Daniels provided Fielding in the dark years after his wife's death, it was clearly of a different and considerably more enjoyable variety than that offered by his sister and his daughter. Fielding got Mary pregnant and master and servant were obliged to marry. At least it negated the need for role play in the bedroom.

QUEENS Called **MARY** or **ANNE**

Mary, Queen of Scots

Mary II

Anne

  Choose one to bed, one to wed and one to behead!

Mary, Queen of Scots

Gentlemen callers beware. Mary was what you might call 'unlucky in love'. She was engaged – aged 5 – to Edward V. He died. She was then engaged to Francis II of France (also aged 5), who died of a poorly ear. Third time lucky? Hardly! Mary married her cousin the Earl of Darnley, who stabbed her secretary David Rizzio to death (fifty-six times!) for an alleged affair before being blown to bits in a suspected murder plot. Having her head cut off by Elizabeth I must have come as a bit of a relief after all that.

Mary II

Mary's father was the notorious James II. He was a Catholic. She was a Protestant. When James was booted off the throne of England for being far too Catholic, Mary claimed the throne, ruled in tandem with her far-too-Protestant husband William of Orange and then went on to grant freedom of worship to everyone, except Catholics. So, if you're the sort of person who's nervous about meeting your date's parents, don't worry about it.

Anne

For all you gentlemen who like footy, fry-ups and like to spell 'England' with an extra syllable, Anne is the girl for you. Anne was proper British. In fact, she invented much of what is considered British today. Under the Act of Union, she turned England and Scotland into one country. She stood up to France and thrashed them in the War of Spanish Succession. She ushered in the two-party political system that we all know and love, sort of inventing the Tory Party in the process. Proper British! But she did outlive all of her children and leave the door open for a hundred or so years of mad German monarchs sitting on the English throne. Traitor!

WIVES of the STUART KINGS

Anne of Denmark

Henrietta Maria

Catherine of Braganza

  Choose one to bed, one to wed and one to behead!

Anne of Denmark

If you are a struggling artist, consider Anne. This Danish wife of James I loved the arts and often spent a ton of money commissioning paintings and spectacular theatrical masques. But if you choose wed and have strong ideas about how to raise your kids, like not letting your wife and queen have anything to do with them because you can't stand her, then reconsider. Anne will stay in bed and starve herself, or refuse to accompany you on that all-important business trip to London to unify Scotland and England. Let her have her way. Anne invented passive aggression.

Henrietta Maria

If you have taken a shine to Henrietta because of the alluring Van Dyke-painted profile picture, then you need to see Henrietta in the flesh before you make a decision. In reality, Henrietta had weirdly long arms and massive teeth. But, during the English Civil War, Henrietta transported guns and ammo from Holland to Bridlington for her hubby Charles I. She unloaded the weapons under fire and even rescued her own pet dog while being shot at by Roundheads. So, if you're the type of guy who subscribes to *Musket and Powder* magazine, choose Henrietta; she's your cherry pie.

Catherine of Braganza

A much-maligned woman. This Portuguese wife of Charles II was initially hated for her Catholicism and falsely implicated in an imagined plot to murder her husband. But the public warmed to her, mainly because of her blind devotion to Charles in spite of all the women he was having it off with. So Charles' numerous public infidelities were actually a form of early reverse psychology designed to warm the public to his wife, and clearly not the selfish antics of a libidinous, randy old tyrant. Just makes you love him all the more, doesn't it?

MISTRESSES of CHARLES II

Hortense Mancini

Barbara Palmer

Lucy Walter

  Choose one to bed, one to wed and one to behead!

Hortense Mancini, Duchess of Mazarin

Mancini was the most favoured niece of the great French clergyman Cardinal Mazarin. But if you're worried that your date won't progress much beyond holding hands, you are in for a mind-bending surprise. This exceedingly tall and beautiful lady liked to dress as a man and danced like a lunatic. She could also fight with sword and gun. Naturally, Charles II fancied the pants off her. But, during your date, try and avoid St James's Park. Mancini is likely to run into, and chuck you over for, Anne Lennard, the king's illegitimate daughter, for whom Mancini had the hots. Don't think about it too much.

Barbara Palmer, 1st Duchess of Cleveland, Countess of Castlemaine

This tall, red-headed lovely with luscious bee-stung lips was the most cruel, foul-mouthed and interfering of all Charles II's mistresses. She once used her influence to destroy the reputation of the 1st Earl of Clarendon and gave birth to Charles II's baby in St James's Palace while the king was on his honeymoon. The diarist John Evelyn called her 'the curse of the nation', while Samuel Peyps thought she was really rather fit. During an evening at the theatre, she once saved a child's life when some scaffolding fell on him. Confused? You can't go wrong with 'fit'.

Lucy Walter

Not much to say about this dark-skinned welsh beauty. Of all the women to catch the king's eye, she was easily the biggest wet blanket. John Evelyn called her 'insipid'. But Charles must have liked her, as rumours abounded that he had married Lucy in secret. She certainly produced his favourite son, who Charles gave the title the Duke of Monmouth. Monmouth was also known as 'the Royal Bastard'. Monmouth would go on to murder a nightwatchman, lead a rebellion and be executed for treason. Be very careful what you call your children.

WIVES of KINGS CALLED GEORGE

Sophia Dorothea
of Celle

Charlotte of
Mecklenburg-Strelitz

Caroline
of Brunswick

  Choose one to bed, one to wed and one to behead!

Sophia Dorothea of Celle

A cautionary tale for anyone thinking of marrying for money. This bad-mannered Hanoverian serial fainter was betrothed to the future King of England purely as a cash match. Sophia and George I hated each other. She said he looked like a pig. He cheated on her. She thought he was a bit thick. He may have had her framed for adultery and certainly locked her up in a castle for thirty years. She died. He banned any public display of grief in Hanover and London. What do you reckon, gents? Nothing like a proportionate response, don't you think?

Charlotte of Mecklenburg-Strelitz

A heart-warming tale for anyone thinking of marrying for love. This Mozart and botany-loving princess was shy and kind to children. Her servants loved her. But Charlotte was considered something of an ugly duckling and no one fancied her. That is until a handsome (ish) George III swept her off her feet, married her and sired fifteen kids. A proper real-life fairy tale, if you ignore the bit where her husband went mad, she couldn't cope and her personality radically altered. So choose wed by all means. Just don't go mad.

Caroline of Brunswick

Quelle surprise! Caroline and her husband the Prince Regent (and future George IV) did not get on. George accused his wife of adultery and banned her from attending his own coronation. Caroline turned up anyway but was refused entry by armed soldiers. George and Caroline were the original ancestors of the type of couple who like to row loudly in public but don't have aggressive make-up sex afterward. In fact, George said they only did it three times in their entire marriage. Caroline said George passed out drunk on their wedding night. See what I mean? It's kicking off again.

VICTORIANA

Queen Victoria

Victoria, Empress of Germany

Princess Helena Victoria

  Choose one to bed, one to wed and one to behead!

Queen Victoria

At sixty-four years, Victoria's was the longest reign in British history. She was Britain's first truly constitutional monarch, the Empress of India and ruler of the world's largest empire. Victoria's public image was austere and severe, mourning her late husband Albert for forty years. Quite an intimidating prospect to wed, bed or even behead? Not really. The key to understanding Victoria is that, in spite of the above, she was just a moody teenage girl at heart. Victoria was an obsessive diarist, never got over her first boyfriend, and, in constantly wearing black, was a bit of a Goth.

Victoria, Empress of Germany

Although fantastically bright (she could read and write aged 5), anybody looking to date Victoria (or 'Vicky', as she preferred to be known) best be aware she was a bit of a mummy's girl. This eldest child of Queen Victoria took the phrase 'Like mother, like daughter' to spooky extremes. Vicky married German royalty (like her mum) and (like her mum) became an empress. Like her mum, Vicky's husband died prematurely, to which Vicky responded by wearing black and mourning him forever and ever, just like her mum. Vicky died in 1901. Didn't her mum do that?

Princess Helena Victoria

If you want to get involved with Helena, you will have to share her with innumerable charitable causes. Queen Victoria's granddaughter supported the YMCA, YWCA, YWCA Women's Auxilliary Force and the Princess Christian's Nursing Home. Helena devoted so much time to her charity work that she never married. Yes, that was definitely the reason Helena never married. Nothing to do with the fact that her two nicknames were 'Snipe', in reference to her rather pointy face and 'Thora', presumably because she looked like a muscle-bound Thora Hird. Is that shallow?

Wed

ZULU WAR HERO Colonel Anthony Durnford had one of the most thwarted love lives of any Victorian soldier. Young Durnford was a religious man with an out–of–control gambling problem. He was an impetuous man who had married in haste and literally repented at leisure when his wife ran off with someone else. Being a religious chap, Durnford gave up the gambling but would or could not divorce his wife. After military service in Ceylon and China, Durnford was posted to South Africa on the eve of the outbreak of the Anglo–Zulu War. He befriended a racially progressive Anglican Bishop named John William Colenso with a virtuous – and really rather hot – daughter named Frances. She was exceedingly attracted to Durnford's courage and honour (Durnford had recently lost the use of his arm in a fight with Hlubi tribesmen and had refused compensation, claiming he 'did not sell his blood'). But most of all, Frances was drawn to Durnford's religion. Durnford and Frances were clearly meant to be together but doomed to be apart because of ... yes ... you've guessed it ... religion!

While Durnford's wife lived, his marriage was still valid in the eyes of God. And being religious, murder was definitely off the cards. So, constrained by their pesky morals, the prospective couple's only chance of being together was to trust in divine providence and hope both of them outlived Durnford's wife. But with a twenty–year age gap between them, Colenso's TB, and Durnford's imminent appointment with thousands of Zulus at the Battle of Isandlwana, that was never going to happen ...

WARRIOR WOMEN

Boudica

Hannah Snell

Charlotte Stanley

Choose one to bed, one to wed and one to behead!

Boudica

If you want to date this ancient world Iceni killing machine, then I hope you like the countryside. A nice day out in London is off the cards. Boudica burned London to the ground and killed all its Roman occupants. Alternatively, if you fancied a day out in Colchester, forget about it. Boudica sacked Colchester, burned it to the ground and killed all its Roman occupants. Boudica also liked hiding things, as the 9th Legion could tell you. She was believed to have ambushed them, killing all the Roman combatants and then removing the bodies. So choose behead. Try it and see what happens.

Hannah Snell

Abandoned by her husband, this eighteenth-century housewife donned men's clothes and joined the marines disguised as a bloke. No one caught on. She went to India and fought at the Battle of Devicotta, where she received eleven wounds to the legs and one right in the family jewels. Luckily, not possessing any jewels, family or otherwise, this hard-as-nails filly avoided a world of pain but provoked some difficult questions from her peers. Somehow Hannah kept her secret (although she revealed it eventually), returned to England and became a pub landlady. I'll bet she didn't need a bouncer.

The Countess of Derby, Charlotte Stanley

This Englishwoman's home literally was her castle. During the Civil War, when her husband was away fighting, Charlotte commanded a detachment of snipers and successfully fought off a Roundhead army who wanted to requisition her stately home. Even when her husband successfully pleaded for her safe passage, stubborn Charlotte stood her ground. At some point during the siege Charlotte threatened to burn her house down and roast herself and her children alive rather than surrender. So, if you plan on marrying Charlotte, you're probably not going to be moving house any time soon.

SUPERNATURAL SIRENS

Mother Shipton

Joanna Southcott

Mary Tofts

  Choose one to bed, one to wed and one to behead!

Mother Shipton

I hope you don't put too much of a premium on looks, because this late fifteenth and early sixteenth-century soothsayer was thought to have been very ugly indeed. She also lived in a cave in Yorkshire. But she did supposedly predict the Great Fire of London. Not bad. She also predicted that the world would end in 1881. It didn't.

Shipton's likeness was said to have provided the prototype for the first pantomime dame. But Mother Shipton would make an awful pantomime dame. She was a prophetess. She'd always know who was behind her, wouldn't she?

Joanna Southcott

This rhyming seer believed herself to be the 'Woman Clothed in the Sun' from the Book of Revelations. She also claimed, aged 64, to be pregnant with the Messiah, and that the world would end in 2004. She wasn't, she wasn't and it didn't. I'm not really selling this one to you, am I? It doesn't help that Joanna doesn't fall into the 'sexy witch' category, but instead resembles your school dinner lady or someone auditioning for *Cranford*. I'm just putting it out there.

Mary Tofts

If you're the type of guy who wants a large family and plenty of pets, then why not combine the two and marry this eighteenth-century Surrey minx? Mary Tofts gave birth to scores of rabbits. That's disgusting, I hear you say. I should think so! All the rabbits were dead on delivery, and some of them not even whole rabbits. It was a hoax, of course, but a very successful one: King George I and many high-ranking medical bods were completely fooled. So how did she do it? Believe me when I say you don't want go there. And don't think too closely about where 'there' actually is …

OUTLAWS

Cutpurse Moll Frith

Joan Phillips

Anne Bonny

  Choose one to bed, one to wed and one to behead!

Cutpurse Moll Frith

Do you really want to go out with someone the courts once called 'a notorious baggage'? You do? Then this badass Jacobean transvestite receiver of stolen goods and occasional pimp might be the girl for you. A trip to the theatre would be an ideal date for Moll, so long as you won't be embarrassed when she jumps on stage and joins in with the production. During drinks afterwards, make sure you toast the health of the reigning monarch: Moll was a staunch Royalist who, legend has it, robbed and wounded a famous Roundhead general on Hounslow Heath. God save the King, beeyatch!

Joan Phillips

Another transvestite outlaw. Joan Phillips dressed as a man and robbed stage coaches at pistol point in the late seventeenth century. Her disguise was so successful that it was said that members of her own gang didn't know she was a woman. The man that finally arrested her didn't even realise she was a woman. If that leads prospective daters to conclude that Joan might be on the ugly side, then they would be wrong. Joan was a stunner. Eventually, she was hanged and her corpse placed in a gibbet and left to rot by the crossroads. Not so pretty now.

Anne Bonny

Only real men need apply for this flame-haired she-pirate. Young Anne was something of a handful. During her youth in the Bahamas, Anne reputedly stabbed a servant and burned down her parents' plantation. As a grown woman, she fought side-by-side with the notorious pirate Calico Jack Rackham. But even Jack didn't meet her exacting standards of machismo: before his execution, Anne criticised Jack, saying, 'If he had fought like a man, he need not have died like a dog'. Ouch!

THEATRICAL FEMALES

Aphra Behn

Nell Gwynn

Elizabeth Barry

  Choose one to bed, one to wed and one to behead!

Aphra Behn

This multilingual writer was the first professional female playwright. Aphra also moonlighted as a spy for Charles II. If you think dating a spy might be glamorous, then think again. Charles forgot to pay her and Aphra was banged up in prison for debt. Aphra's best remembered plays include *The Rover* and *The Forced Marriage*. But she also wrote *The Emperor of the Moon*, which is considered the antecedent of the traditional Christmas pantomime. Feminist icon, or the harbinger of annual theatrical Armageddon? You decide.

Nell Gwynn

An inspirational tale for every theatre usher who ever dreamed of making it big on the stage. Restoration saucepot Nell Gwynn started out selling oranges but ended up as the great comic actress of her age. In order to achieve her goal, she only had to sleep with an actor, a lord and the King of England. But that was all by-the-by. Nell was a genuinely talented actress and great fun to hang out with. When mistaken by an excited crowd for the Catholic Duchess of Portland, Nell calmed and corrected the crowd with these words, 'Pray good people, be civil, I am the *Protestant* whore'. She said it.

Elizabeth Barry

Legend has it that that Barry couldn't act a lick until the lecherous aristocrat Lord Rochester trained her up for a bet. Certainly, by the end of her life, she was one of the most revered thespians of the seventeenth century. But for those shallow gents who fancy the idea of dating a glamorous celebrity, a word of caution. In the parlance of the time, Barry was considered something of a 'munter'. Unless she was on stage that is; then she was considered a radiant beauty. Rochester obviously found her attractive: she had his baby.

LADIES of the NIGHT

Mother Needham

Sally Salisbury

Mother Douglas

  Choose one to bed, one to wed and one to behead!

Mother Needham

Immortalised by Hogarth in his series of moralistic sketches *The Harlot's Progress*, Elizabeth Needham was one of the most ruthless brothel-keepers and procurers of prostitutes in Georgian London's West End. Needham targeted naive country girls new to the capital. Once recruited, Needham would make them hire their working clothes from her, get them into debt and then kick them out on to the street when they were too old to earn. Needham also worked closely with the notorious Colonel Francis Charteris, known to his intimates as the Rapemaster General. Needham would supply Charteris with girls. What's not to love?

Sally Salisbury

This popular prostitute worked in some of the most exclusive brothels in London. Sally would guarantee you a decent night out in London's West End. But avoid the opera. Sally once stabbed the aristocrat John Finch with a dining fork during an argument over opera tickets. But even if your date lands you stabbed-up and in A&E, you won't hold it against her. John Finch forgave Sally. It didn't stop her getting a £100 fine, and a year in prison. Interestingly, Sally initially embarked on a life of whoredom after a career in textiles failed when she lost a piece of lace and ran away. Bit of an overreaction.

Mother Douglas

This Scottish brothel-keeper was known affectionately as 'Mother of the Bawds'. So, if you have to date a professional procurer of prostitutes, you could do a lot worse than spend a night in Douglas' famously high-end Covent Garden emporium. She treated her whores well, provided condoms and ran a nice restaurant. There was even a doctor on hand to treat any syphilitic clientele. Now that's what I call multitasking.

Behead

THOMAS MORE AND OLIVER CROMWELL were both expert practitioners of the arcane party game known as 'cranial pass the parcel'. The rules were simple. Firstly, in order to play, you needed to have been beheaded and your skull displayed in a prominent position in London. Secondly, the head needed to have been reclaimed by either a grieving relative (More), or a passerby when the supporting spike holding the head aloft snaps in a freak storm (Cromwell). Thirdly, the head needed to be passed from person to person until it either disappeared completely from history, or was reburied with all the proper ceremony. The head that remained in circulation the longest was the winner.

So: Thomas More *v.* Oliver Cromwell. Who won?

Thomas More's head was retrieved by his daughter Margaret Roper in 1535. Margaret died in 1544 and was thought to have been buried along with her father's head. She wasn't.

More's head was last spotted under famous poet (and distant ancestor) John Donne's bed. Donne died in 1631, and bequeathed the head to a relative. Don't know what happened to More's head after that.

Crowell's corpse, meanwhile, was dug up and beheaded by Charles II in 1658. Cromwell's head fell off its spiky perch in 1685, and spent the next few centuries disappearing and resurfacing periodically. Its custodians included an actor and a Georgian collector of Cromwellian memorabilia. Cromwell was eventually reunited with his body in 1960, when both were buried at Sidney Sussex College, Cambridge.

So, I think that you will agree that Crowell wins cranial pass the parcel by considerably more than a nose, although I believe Crowell's nose had rotted off long before 1960.

The **BRONTË SISTERS**

Anne Brontë

Emily Brontë

Charlotte Brontë

  Choose one to bed, one to wed and one to behead!

Anne Brontë

If your dating preference is a thoughtful young lady with a vivid imagination, then Anne is definitely your girl. Despite writing such chick-lit classics as *Agnes Grey* and *The Tenant of Wildfell Hall*, Anne also liked to dabble in sci-fi and fantasy having, in her teens, created the imaginary world of Gondel (check it out, it's better than Harry Potter). But Anne's make-believe wonderings were tempered by a stay-at-home nature. Anne didn't get out much. She barely left Yorkshire. In fact, the most exciting place she ever visited was Scarborough, where she died of TB, at 2 p.m., aged 29.

Emily Brontë

If your dating preference is a thoughtful young lady with a vivid imagination, then Emily is definitely your girl. Despite writing such chick-lit classics as *Wuthering Heights*, Emily also liked to dabble in sci-fi and fantasy having, in her teens, created the imaginary world of Gondel (check it out, it's better than Harry Potter). Hang on a minute! Wasn't that Anne's profile? It makes no odds. Emily and Anne's biography is almost identical, including dying of a respiratory illness at 2 p.m., although Emily was aged 30. So it doesn't really matter which one you date, does it?

Charlotte Brontë

By far the most colourful of the Brontë sisters, Charlotte succeeded in getting out of Yorkshire, saw the world (or at least Brussels), learned German and French and studied music. She even managed to get herself married and write the chick-lit classic *Jane Eyre*. She wrote some other stuff that nobody reads these days (*Shirley*, *The Professor*) but they were mostly pervier variations on *Jane Eyre*, so best not to bother with those. More importantly, Charlotte managed to avoid dying of a respiratory illness at 2 p.m., aged 29 or 30. She died in childbirth, aged 38.

MISTRESSES

Lady Emma
Hamilton

Georgiana
Cavendish

Lady Caroline
Lamb

  Choose one to bed, one to wed and one to behead!

Lady Emma Hamilton

Pilloried as the scarlet woman of Georgian England for getting off with Horatio Nelson, there was much to pity and admire about Mrs Hamilton. Her own marriage was hardly ideal: Emma was effectively given to her elderly husband by a former lover. When Emma was sent to meet him, she actually thought she was going away on holiday. To his credit, her husband didn't seem to mind that much when Emma started seeing Nelson. Not great wife material, then? No, but definitely great mistress material: Emma had a reputation for being faithful to all the men she ever betrayed her husband with. A most ingenious paradox.

Georgiana Cavendish

The Duchess of Devonshire had a famously unhappy marriage. Despite being beautiful, intelligent and politically savvy, as well as a novelist and the subject of paintings by Reynolds and Gainsborough, Georgiana's famously repressed husband wouldn't touch her with a barge pole. So Georgiana scandalously sought comfort in the arms of Whig politician Charles Grey. But forget all that. If you're considering dating Georgiana, then your main concern ought to be the size of her wig. It was massive. So wherever you choose to take her, make sure the ceiling's really high and that there are no naked flames on the chandeliers.

Lady Caroline Lamb

Whatever you do, don't dump her. This wife to future prime minister Lord Melbourne became Byron's most clingy mistress and then went properly bunny-boiler mental when the Romantic poet gave her the old heave-ho. She published poems about him, wrote a novel about him and even visited his house when he wasn't there and wrote a personal message in one of his books. Lady Lamb was the one who described Lord Byron as 'mad, bad and dangerous to know'. Really?! Physician, heal thyself.

SOLDIERS' WIVES

Sarah Churchill

Frances Nelson

Catherine Wellesley

  Choose one to bed, one to wed and one to behead!

Sarah Churchill

The wife of England's greatest general was also a close friend of Queen Anne. When Queen Anne was merely Princess Anne, Sarah advanced her cause to the reigning monarch William of Orange. This ensured that Sarah and Anne would be BFFs. Consequently, Sarah had a lot of juice and even influenced government policy. But prospective daters beware: Sarah had a habit of wanting her own way all of the time, and eventually offended Anne when the latter's husband died, making Anne's former BFF her current IFBFFWHTTTTHRHTPHSUASG (Irritating Former Best Friend Forever Who Had The Temerity To Tell Her Royal Highness To Pull Her Socks Up And Stop Grieving).

Frances Nelson

Wed! Wed! Wed! You could not find a more devoted wife in Georgian England. Admiral Nelson's Mrs put up with his long working hours, nursed him when he lost his arm in combat, tolerated his humiliating and public affair with Emma Hamilton and looked after his ailing dad. Even when Nelson was dead, Frances carried a miniature of the war hero around with her. Which just goes to prove that Nelson was more of a man dead, with one eye and a missing arm, than most physically intact mortal males are ever likely to be.

Catherine Wellesley

Oh dear. This is the woman that the Duke of Wellington made wait for ten years and then called ugly behind her back. At least he married her, although goodness knows why. They slept in separate rooms and when the Peninsular War kicked off Catherine didn't see her husband until all the fighting was over. When she did, he was appalled that she had put on a few pounds. Whoever said absence makes the heart grow fonder wants a kick in the plums.

DO-GOODERS

Elizabeth Fry

Florence Nightingale

Mary Seacole

  Choose one to bed, one to wed and one to behead!

Elizabeth Fry

This is the lady on the £5 note sitting on a stool surrounded by women and small kids. What's that all about? Well, the women and small kids are female convicts in Newgate Prison and the lady is Elizabeth Fry. Elizabeth ('Betsy') Fry was a Quaker who used her wealth and influence to visit prisons and bend Parliament and Queen Victoria's ear about how appalling conditions were for the nation's convicts. A good woman? Undoubtedly. But she replaced that fantastic picture of the Duke of Wellington on the old fivers, which makes her a bit of a bitch in my opinion.

Florence Nightingale

Fancy dating a saint? Well, Florence comes pretty close. The Lady of the Lamp brought comfort and hope to the wounded and dying in the Crimean War and introduced practices that transformed the face of nursing to this day – and all of this with only three months' training. Now, about that three months' training! More soldiers popped their clogs under Florence's care than before she arrived. So perhaps she isn't an actual saint. But she was a nurse who managed to stay sexually chaste all her days. Surely that's some form of miracle?

Mary Seacole

This well-travelled Jamaican taught herself nursing, went to the Crimea and built a hospital out of scrap metal and bits of crap. She called it the 'British Hotel' and the soldiers loved it. That's probably because Mary sold them booze. Mary was very brave. She treated the wounded under fire and was the first nurse into Sevastapol when the city fell. She got into trouble though, when she looted a bell, a candle and a painting – and Florence Nightingale didn't particularly like her. But who cares: resurrect her and put her in charge of the NHS.

AUTHORS

Jane Austen

Elizabeth Gaskell

George Eliot

  Choose one to bed, one to wed and one to behead!

Jane Austen

We can provide prospective daters with virtually no useful information about the author of *Pride and Prejudice*, due to her brother and sister burning most of her private correspondence. We do know that in her youth she hung out with a scandalous Irishman named Tom Lefroy, whom she was eventually banned from seeing. We don't know what they got up to, but a surviving letter of Jane's confesses, 'I am almost afraid to tell you how my Irish friend and I behaved. Imagine to yourself everything most profligate in the way of dancing and sitting down together.' Slaaaaag!

Elizabeth Gaskell

If you want to meet the stars, then Lizzy's your girl. Elizabeth Gaskell was a bit of name-dropper, hanging out with the likes of Charles Dickens, Charlotte Brontë and Florence Nightingale. She even wrote Brontë's biography. But Liz is best known for the novel *Cranford*, based on her early life growing up in the Cheshire town of Knutsford. *Cranford* was a largely forgotten novel until the BBC adapted it a few years back. Knutsford is a much funnier name than Cranford, though. Gaskell should have called her novel *Knutsford*. Perhaps it would have shifted a few more copies.

George Eliot

If Jane Austen isn't racy enough for you and Elizabeth Gaskell is too blind to the comic possibilities of the word 'Knutsford', why not consider George Eliot? Her real name was Mary Ann Evans. She was a stay-at-home daddy's girl until her father died. Then she went proper mental, assumed a man's name to pen weighty novels, wrote radical political journalism, lived with a married man and – when she'd worn him out – shacked up with a young fella twenty years her junior. If you don't want her, get out of my way – I'll have me some of that!

SCIENTISTS

Mary Anning

Ada Lovelace

Elizabeth Garrett Anderson

  Choose one to bed, one to wed and one to behead!

Mary Anning

What self-respecting unreconstructed boy/man doesn't love dinosaurs? If I'm describing you, then consider Mary Anning. This unschooled, self-educated woman lived in Lyme Regis and had a diviner's talent for finding dinosaur bones in the chalky cliff face. Mary Anning was the first person to find a plesiosaur. Who knows what Jurassic treasures you might find on a date with Mary? And if you find a particularly rare and valuable specimen, you could always buy it off her and take all the credit for the discovery, just like the nineteenth-century scientific establishment did. It's not unethical. A hundred repressed Victorian palaeontologists can't be wrong.

Ada Lovelace

Intimidated by smart women? Then stay well clear. This illegitimate daughter of the poet Byron was frighteningly intelligent, with an intellect over a century ahead of its time. Aged 17, Ada Lovelace met Charles Babbage and improved his design for the 'Analytical Engine' – the Victorian antecedent of the modern computer. Ada's main contribution to Babbage's design was to programme the machine to repeat instructions – that, and teaching Babbage that if the Analytical Engine ever broke down, he could make it work again by switching it off and then switching it back on.

Elizabeth Garrett Anderson

The hottest thing to come out of Whitechapel since Jack the Ripper, Elizabeth Anderson was the first woman to qualify as a doctor. And all she had to do to achieve this exalted position was apply to Middlesex Hospital as a nurse, sneak into all male classes, exploit a loophole that allowed her to study under the Society of Apocatheries and then conclude her education in France. Eventually her battles earned women complete acceptance in the medical profession. Either that or the fact that – post-immigration – English society discovered another put-upon group to fear, distrust and persecute within their own medical communities. It's what we do.

GOTHS

Ann Radcliffe

Charlotte Dacre

Mary Shelley

  Choose one to bed, one to wed and one to behead!

Ann Radcliffe

The grand matriarch of the gothic novel, Radcliffe gave much legitimacy to a previously disreputable genre. She was very reclusive, retired at the peak of her success and probably won't show up for your date. But Radcliffe's legacy is enormous. She invented 'explained supernaturalism', which means that the monster or ghost in the story is not really a monster or a ghost. This was a technique that found its fullest expression in *The Hound of the Baskervilles* and any episode of *Scooby-Doo*.

Charlotte Dacre

Never heard of her? Apparently Dacre wrote some of the most sensuous and assertive women in the gothic cannon, most famously in the novel *Zofloya*. Never heard of it? You should have. This dark tale of interracial sexual tension was branded as pornography in England but didn't cause so much as a ripple of disgust in France. Byron didn't like Dacre and was thought to have rubbished her in his poem 'English Bards and Scottish Reviewers'. Forget Byron and consider Dacre. Millions of randy Frenchman can't be wrong.

Mary Shelley

The author of *Frankenstein* could have been the subject of gothic novel: Mary's mum died when she was just over a week old, while Mary herself had an affair with a famous married poet whose wife killed herself. Mary married the poet and had a daughter who died and then the poet drowned. In the middle of all this misery and woe Mary wrote *Frankenstein*, when it came to her in a nightmare during the most debauched and sinister party in literary history. Oh, and she died of a brain tumour. Forget the others and dust off your copy of *Interview with the Vampire*; this woman was proper Goth.

The **PRE-RAPHAELITE SISTERHOOD**

Jane Morris

Georgiana Burne-Jones

Effie Gray

  Choose one to bed, one to wed and one to behead!

Jane Morris

Ever fancied dating a model? Jane Morris was spotted by Pre-Raphaelite painters Dante Gabriel Rossetti and Edward Burne-Jones whilst attending the theatre. She modelled for them both, but married the painter William Morris. Jane was formally uneducated but took advantage of opportunities to improve herself and became something of an academic polymath and possible inspiration for Eliza Doolittle. She later had an affair with Rossetti but the pair fell out due to Rossetti's excessive drug intake.

Considering choosing bed? If you're married, then you've got nothing to fear from Jane. But if you're partial to laudanum, or a bit of the old charlie …

Georgiana Burne-Jones

Ever fancied dating a model? Stick to just dating. On the surface Georgiana looks like good wife material: she was kind and gentle, and she married her childhood sweetheart, the painter Edward Burne-Jones, after a long engagement. But Georgiana's parents were strict Methodists who didn't let her attend the theatre, rendering their daughter a ticking time bomb of religion-induced repression. Once married, Georgiana had a wild fling with Mary Zambaco, the model who posed for John William Waterhouse's painting of the Homeric sorceress Circe. Parents, this is what happens when you don't allow your children to go to the panto.

Effie Gray

Ever fancied marrying a model? Then for goodness sake, consummate the marriage. This might seem an obvious thing to say, but Effie Gray's husband, the art critic John Ruskin, didn't have sex with his wife at all in the first five years of their marriage. Five years! The marriage was annulled and Effie wed the painter John Millais instead. The fallout from the scandal earned Effie Grey the disapproval of Queen Victoria, who banned her from her presence. So choose wed and bed. The poor girl's earned it. Five years!

ACTRESSES

Marie Lloyd

Lillie Langtry

Ellen Terry

  Choose one to bed, one to wed and one to behead!

Marie Lloyd

Fancy a cock-er-nee knees up in front of the old Joanna? Choose Marie. She pretty much invented it. This 'Queen of the Music Hall' and original East Ender made songs like 'My Old Man' and 'A Little of What You Fancy' world famous. As well as prefiguring the careers of Chas and Dave, Marie pre-empted the *Carry On* films by taking seemingly innocent lyrics and making them sound very rude indeed. She once got in a lot of trouble for singing a very suggestive rendition of Tennyson's 'Come into the Garden, Maud' without changing any of the words. I don't get it.

Lillie Langtry

This Jersey girl and one-time mistress of the Prince of Wales (the future Edward VII) was the most glamorous actress of the nineteenth century. Everybody fancied her. Even Queen Victoria's youngest had to be told off for having a picture of her above his bed. But if you are considering a date, then beware of stalkers. Roy Bean, the famous American hanging judge, never even met Lillie but was so obsessed with her that he named a town after her and sent her a live bear as a present. A live bear? Would you have to sign for that?

Ellen Terry

This Victorian actress was one of the true theatrical greats of her era. She played many Shakespearean roles and acted opposite Henry Irving and Herbert Beerbohm Tree, while George Bernard Shaw was a big fan. She earned loads, netting £200 a week when on tour. But Terry's love life was predictably messy. Considering marriage? A word of caution. Ellen married a famous painter who painted her. Ellen married a famous architect who built her a house. Do you see a pattern forming here? Now I ain't saying she's a gold digga …

ADVENTURESSES

Lady Hester Stanhope

Mary Kingsley

Gertrude Bell

  Choose one to bed, one to wed and one to behead!

Lady Hester Stanhope

This niece and former secretary of Pitt the Younger liked wearing men's clothes ever since she was shipwrecked off the coast of Rhodes. Anyone wanting to date Lady Stanhope would have to get used to addressing her as 'Queen Hester'. Anyone considering marriage would have to like large deserted monasteries: Hester lived in three of them. If she sounds delightfully eccentric, then remember that there is a thin line separating eccentric from completely cuckoo. Hester believed she was destined to marry a messiah and once smashed a priceless statue to pieces because it wasn't hidden treasure.

Mary Kingsley

Charles Kingsley (Mary's dad) wrote *The Water Babies*. Mary Kingsley (Charles' daughter) educated herself, went to Africa, discovered three new species of fish, was nearly eaten by a crocodile, hung out with cannibals, climbed Mount Cameroon and proved herself an outstanding and progressive anthropologist. If that sounds a bit too 'women's lib' for your tastes, then don't fret. Bizarrely, Mary Kingsley didn't believe women should have the vote. She also defended the right of a man to have more than one wife. Bingo! I think I've just described the perfect woman.

Gertrude Bell

Had this tall, elegantly dressed, whip-smart woman not become one of the great political architects of modern Iraq, she would have been remembered as the best female mountaineer of the early twentieth century. Gertrude once survived fifty-three hours stuck on the north-east face of the Finsteraarhorn in a brutal blizzard. That aside, Gertrude Bell taught herself Persian, knew T.E. Lawrence and was a rare English diplomat, beloved by the Arabs. You'd have thought men would be queuing up. They weren't. Gertrude Bell died unmarried, childless, miserable and alone. So choose wed or I'll track you down myself and chin you.

Behead

IF YOU EVER have to be beheaded, you could do a lot worse than get on the wrong side of Francis Drake. He once ordered the beheading of a member of his own crew during his legendary circumnavigation of the globe. And he couldn't have been nicer about it.

The victim in question was Thomas Doughty, a nobleman. (Drake had yet to be knighted.) The two men had been friends before the voyage, but once the small fleet set sail, Doughty immediately took umbrage at being given orders by the socially inferior Drake and began to undermine him. Drake was obliged to dismiss a ship's master. Doughty grumbled about it to his men. Drake suspected Doughty's brother of theft. Doughty grumbled about it to his men. Doughty and his brother claimed to possess supernatural powers, telling their men that they could summon demonic lions or bears which, in itself, was something of a red rag to the Puritan Drake. When Doughty made the mistake of threatening Drake, it was the beginning of the end. But Drake was nice about it. He moved Doughty from ship to ship in order to curtail his seditious rumblings, but wherever Drake placed him, Doughty would stir the manure. Enough was enough. Drake put Doughty on trial for witchcraft and mutiny.

Doughty was found guilty and sentenced to death. The execution was efficient: his head was removed with one clean lop. But before Doughty's death, Drake treated the mutineer to a slap-up meal, a lovely communion service, a farewell embrace and the promise that no retaliation would be meted out to Doughty's followers. What a guy! With enemies like these, who needs friends?

FEMMES FATALES

Mary Bateman

Eliza Fenning

Marie Manning

  Choose one to bed, one to wed and one to behead!

Mary Bateman

Mary was also known as the 'Yorkshire Witch'. Don't worry. Mary wasn't really a witch. She was a con woman who pretended to tell people's fortunes and free them from the influence of evil spirits. Mary was also a murderer, having killed a man by feeding him poisoned pudding. She was eventually hanged for her crimes and her body was placed in a gibbet. If you're still interested, you can check out Mary for yourself if you wish: her skeleton is on display in a museum in Leeds. She's lost a bit of weight though …

Eliza Fenning

If Eliza asks you if you want to eat out or stay in for a nice home-cooked meal, then for goodness sake, eat out. Elizabeth achieved notoriety in 1849 for allegedly killing an entire family by serving them poisoned dumplings. I say 'allegedly', though she was convicted of murder and hanged. However, 10,000 people turned up at her funeral protesting her innocence and Charles Dickens didn't think she did it. Still, best be on the cautious side. Avoid dim sum or Jamaican restaurants. Go to the pictures instead – but don't share your popcorn.

Marie Manning

She definitely did it. This plump perpetrator of the 'Bermondsey Horror' conspired with her husband to murder Patrick O'Connor, a moneylender and mutual friend, burying O'Connor in their kitchen before looting his property. Marie Manning wore black lace at her hanging, and sales of black lace were believed to have plummeted as a consequence. Charles Dickens got loads of mileage out of the Bermondsey Horror, though. He wrote a famous account of the Mannings' execution for a newspaper and used Marie as the basis for Mademoiselle Hortense in his novel *Bleak House*. Some people will do absolutely anything to get into one of that man's books.

FEISTY FEMALES

Cordelia of Britain

Mary Wollstonecraft

Grace Darling

  Choose one to bed, one to wed and one to behead!

Cordelia of Britain

Apparently the nice daughter in Shakespeare's *King Lear* actually existed, and was pretty feisty. King Lear also existed and actually was deposed by two scheming daughters. Cordelia and Lear fled to Gaul, returned with an army and sorted out their unruly relatives. In the play, it ends badly for Lear, who dies a broken man. In reality, it ended badly for Cordelia, who killed herself when deposed by her nephews. Little is known about Cordelia, including how long she lived. But I'll bet that her lifespan was considerably shorter than the length of an average production of *King Lear*.

Mary Wollstonecraft

If Mary was a stick of rock, you could have cut her in half and found the word 'feisty' running all the way through her. Mary left her repressive and brutal father, had a daughter out of wedlock, married the man that sort of invented anarchism, had another daughter who went on to write *Frankenstein*, and sort of invented feminism herself when she wrote *A Vindication of the Rights of Women*. But the feistiest thing Mary ever did was to die, allowing her salacious, uncensored autobiography to be published. It's proper filthy – or so I'm told.

Grace Darling

Geordie lass Grace Darling only did one thing that could be qualified as feisty – but what a thing! Grace lived in a lighthouse and rowed out in stormy seas to a stricken steamship that was coming apart on the rocks and rescued a bunch of survivors. Her single heroic act was commemorated in literature, poetry and art. Except Grace didn't do any actual rowing: her dad did it all. Grace sat in the back and steered. Unbelievable! I just feel bad for all these boys who have a thing about girls with well-muscled backs and brawny forearms.

IRON LADIES

Jeanette Jerome

Nancy Astor

Lady Cynthia Mosley

Choose one to bed, one to wed and one to behead!

Jeanette Jerome
aka Lady Randolph Churchill

The original Jenny from the block. This beautiful Brooklyn-born lovely dabbled in playwriting and publishing before marrying into the Churchill family and sculpting the careers of husband Randolph and soon-to-be-legendary son Winston. It was a task Jenny achieved by a mixture of formidable political savvy and sleeping with anybody that might advance the family cause. Jenny's little black book was awesome, containing the phone numbers of Otto von Bismarck and the Prince of Wales. Why she'd want to put herself on the market and date you is anybody's guess.

Nancy Astor

This tiny American tomboy with penetrating blue eyes was the first female MP in the House of Commons. Married to a Tory politician, Nancy won a by-election when her husband vacated his position to join the House of Lords. Nancy was a consummate campaigner, charming even the most hostile crowd. However, Nancy was also a bit of Nazi sympathiser. Could you be a bit of a Nazi sympathiser? Nancy could. On the one hand, she criticised Hitler for his poor record on equal rights, but on the other, she gave him a free pass on his treatment of Jews.

Lady Cynthia Mosley

This Derbyshire lass and MP for the Labour Party married her first boyfriend. Having never been out with anybody before, Lady Cynthia remained true to her first love all the days of her life. How sweet and reassuring. Not really: the love in question was Oswald Mosley, who was not only England's most prominent fascist but also a king-sized adulterer. Mosley had affairs with Cynthia's sister, Cynthia's step-mum and Diana Mitford. And after all of that Oswald still had enough energy to go out and pick fights with Jews in London's East End.

Behead

IT MIGHT SURPRISE YOU to know that as late as the nineteenth century, there was still the odd Englishman who believed that beheading was occasionally necessary. But unlike the godless, post–revolutionary French, Victorian Englishmen would only behead in moderation and always felt bad about it afterwards.

Second Lieutenant Henry Hugh Clifford won the Victoria Cross for chopping a Russian soldier's head off. The deed was done in the Crimean War, during the Battle of Inkerman. Clifford had led a charge against Russian lines and was involved in intense hand–to–hand combat when something went wrong with his revolver. Clifford drew his sword. A Russian soldier tried to bayonet him, so Clifford chopped his arm off. Another Russian soldier tried to get out of Clifford's way. Clifford chopped his head off. Almost immediately afterwards, about fifteen Russian soldiers surrendered to Clifford. Well you would, wouldn't you?

After the battle, Clifford was walking amongst the injured prisoners. The Russian whose arm Clifford had severed called him over, and the two exchanged pleasantries. The prisoner laughed, and Henry Clifford shook the man's remaining hand. Clifford was deeply moved by the encounter and later expressed regret that he had no money to give the one-armed soldier. He later marvelled that he had ever been so violent and doubted whether he could replicate such brutality in cold blood.

IMAGE SOURCES

The History Press

Louis VIII; Edward, the Black Prince; John of Gaunt; Oliver Cromwell; Ernest Augustus; Archbishop Laud; Richard Grenville, from the Pascall's 'Worthies of Devon' series (1927); Dr John Dee; William Blake; Richard Burbage; Dick Turpin; Major General Sir Arthur Wellington; William Wordsworth; portrait of Keats on his grave; John Wesley; John Howard; Robert Stevenson; Isambard Kingdom Brunel; Thomas Bauch; James Hudson Taylor; Charles Dickens; Speke, from the frontispiece to his *Journey of the Discovery of the Source of the Nile*; Anne Neville; Anne of Denmark, from the coronation record number of the *Illustrated London News*; Empress Matilda; Isabella, the She–Wolf, from the coronation number of the *Illustrated London News* (1935); Elizabeth Woodville; Lady Margaret Beaufort; Joan Phillips; Aphra Behn, from *The Works of Aphra Behn*; George Elliot (*The works of George Eliot*, Vol. 18, 1910); Anne Bonny; Boudicca; Joanna Southcott; Mary Bateman; Eliza Fenning; Maria Manning; Hogarth engravings of Mother Douglas and Mother Needham; Barbara Palmer, Duchess of Cleveland and Lucy Walter, from Grammont's *Memoirs*; Sophia Dorothea, from Ogden's 1902 'Guinea Gold'; Lady Hester Stanhope, from the first volume of her *Memoirs*; Mary Kingsley, *Black and White Magazine* (1897); Marie Lloyd from 'Celebrities of Music Hall'; Elizabeth Barry, *Annals of the English Stage* (1888); the Brontës, from the frontispiece to *Brontë Poems: Selections from Charlotte, Emily, Anne & Branwell Brontë* (1915); Mary Anning, *Natural History Magazine* (April 1935); Grace Darling, from Scott's edition of *Grace Darling, Heroine of the Farne Islands* (1887); Hannah Snell; Moll Frith; Sally Salisbury; Mrs Gaskell, from Haldane's *Mrs Gaskell and her Friends* (1930); Lady Caroline Lamb; Lady Catherine Packenham, later Lady Wellesley, from Major Arthur Griffiths' *Wellington and Waterloo* (1898); The Countess of Derby, from Lodge's *Portraits of Illustrious Personages of Great Britain*; Elizabeth Garrett Anderson, from the biography written by her daughter; Mrs Frances Nelson, from Mahan's *Life of Nelson*; Jane Morris and Georgiana Burne–Jones, from *Memorials of Edward Burne-Jones* (1904); Effie Gray, from *Life of and Letters of Sir John Everett Millais by his Son* (1900); Cordelia of Britain; Matilda of Flanders; Matilda of Scotland; Adeliza of Louvain; Matilda of Boulogne; Mary Tofts; Berengaria of Navarre; Isabella of Angoulême; Mother Shipton.

Kings and Queens of England (1935)

William I; William II; Henry I; Stephen I; Henry II; Richard I; John; Henry III; Edward I; Edward II; Edward III; Richard II; Henry VI; Edward IV; Edward V; Catherine of Aragon; Anne Boleyn; Catherine Howard; Henrietta Maria; Catherine of Braganza; Charlotte of Mecklenburg-Strelitz; Queen Caroline; Queen Victoria.

The Portrait Book of our Kings and Queens, 1066–1911 (1911)

Henry IV; Henry V; Richard III; Henry VII; Henry VIII; Edward VI; James I; Charles I; Charles II; James II; William III; George I; George II; George III; George IV; Mary I; Elizabeth I; Mary II; Queen Anne.

Celebrities of British History (1935)

William IV; Thomas Becket; Shakespeare; Sir Francis Drake; John Milton; Sir Walter Raleigh; Christopher Wren; John Churchill, Duke of Marlborough; General Wolfe; Robert Walpole; William Pitt the Elder; Lord Byron; Isaac Newton; William Gladstone; Benjamin Disraeli; Horatio Nelson; Captain James Cook; David Livingstone; Thomas More; Samuel Pepys; Mary, Queen of Scots; Lady Hamilton; Elizabeth Fry; Sarah Churchill, Duchess of Marlborough.

Getty Images

Portrait of nobleman, perhaps Christopher Marlowe, 9585 (De Agostini Picture Library at Getty Images, 162279765).

Library of Congress

Ben Jonson (LC-USZ62–138132); Kean as Richard III (LC-USZ62–120971); Henry Irving (LC-USZ62–105316); Claude Duval (LC-USZ62–13515); highwayman representing John Nevison (LC-USZ62–28575); Cranmer (LC-DIG-det-4a26507); Inigo Jones (LC-USZ62–105617); Charles Babbage (LC-USZ62–66023); Charles Darwin (LC-DIG-ggbain–03485); T.E. Lawrence (LC-DIG-ppmsca–19413); Robert Falcon Scott (LC-USZ62–5995); Oscar Wilde (LC-DIG-ppmsca–07757); Rudyard Kipling (LC-USZ62–101366); Richard Burton (LC-USZ61–236); Jane Seymour (LC-USZ62–128486); Anne of Cleves (LC-USZ62–128712); Hortense Manzini. (LC-DIG-det-4a25025); Queen Victoria's family (LC-DIG-pga–02489); Georgiana Cavendish; Florence Nightingale (LC-USZ62–5877); Jane Austen (LC-USZ62–103529); Lillie Langtry (LC-USZ62–92567); Ellen Terry (LC-USZ62–96552); Gertrude Bell (LC-DIG-matpc-08277); Lady Randolph Churchill (LC-DIG-ggbain–14381); Lady Astor (LC-DIG-ggbain–34107); Lady Cynthia Moseley (LC-DIG-ggbain–38928); Mary Wollstonecraft (LC-USZ62–64309).

Other

Sir John Soane, statue at the Bank of England (with thanks to T. Denzer); William Adams (rendered from the original woodblock portrait by Nesnad); William Pitt the Younger (Shutterstock, 81840889); Lord Melbourne (Shutterstock, 81840829); Eleanor of Aquitaine (Elanor Gamgee); Catherine Parr (Shutterstock, 86442169); Lady Jane Grey (Shutterstock, 81841840); William Wilberforce (Shutterstock, 81840883); Ada Lovelace (Courtesy of the Ada Initiative and Colin Adams, through Wikimedia Commons).